Funding the Family Business

A Handbook for Raising Personal Support

Myles Wilson

© Myles Wilson

Edited by Annabel Warburg

Design © Adrian & Rika Baggett, design@adrianbaggett.demon.co.uk

Illustrations © Ange Moyler

Biblical Principles exercises developed by Chris Richardson

Sample support album designed by Martin Russell

Cover design by Ange Moyler

For information on the services offered by Stewardship, including *Funding the Family Business* updates and seminar details, visit www.stewardship.org.uk

All rights reserved. No part of this publication may be reproduced, stored on a retrieval system, or transmitted in any form, or by any means, electronic, mechanical, photocopying, recording or otherwise without the prior permission of the publisher.

First published in 2006

ISBN: 978-0-9553320-0-5 / 0-9553320-0-1

Published by Stewardship
Registered Charity No. 234714

Unless otherwise stated, all Biblical quotes are from the New International Version, by kind permission of the publishers.

"This book should be required reading for anyone having to raise support. Myles has done a brilliant job in giving us this resource. Would you like to help someone who is raising support? Start by giving them a copy of this unique book. Raising support can be harder than getting a PhD, and if you are not willing to pray hard and work, forget it! This book will help you in the process."

George Verwer, Founder, Operation Mobilisation

"Working with Wycliffe Bible Translators for over 20 years, our support had fallen from its previously good position to a level that caused us to seriously considering resigning. With Myles' help, we realised that we had adjusted to many other cultures, but not to that of younger Christians. They need to be involved in a totally new way. And they want to be involved, and to give financially. Myles helped us see how we could combine our faith in God's provision with the right approach to supporters of a new generation. Funding the Family Business is an absolute must-read for those who want to raise not just support, but supporters for our Father's work."

Steve and Johanna Pillinger, Wycliffe Bible Translators

"For over a decade Myles has trained hundreds of Youth for Christ staff in raising personal support. His Biblical, clear, humorous and practical approach has been extremely effective – this is found in Funding the Family Business. It will radically change your approach to money and ministry. Buy it, read it, use it!"

Roy Crowne, National Director, British Youth for Christ

"Having worked with YWAM for some years and now being in so-called 'normal' jobs, we have seen both sides of this process. What often surprises and frustrates us now is how difficult people make it for us to give and become involved in their exciting ministries. Leaving it up to us to fill out forms or guess what level of support they need. We are delighted that Myles has put his experience and wisdom into print in Funding the Family Business. This fantastic resource will help those who raise support do a better job of building true partnership with their supporters – and that will make it easier for givers to give."

Mark and Tracey Brooks, Gloucester

"I am delighted that Myles has put his years of experience into print. Funding the Family Business isn't just about finding financial supporters. It is about building teams of givers and receivers, working together for the extension of God's Kingdom, a true partnership in the gospel. Giving a copy of this book to all their staff will be one of the best investments any mission could make."

Martin Lee, Executive Director, Global Connections

CONTENTS

Preface – Why I have come to write this book ... 1

Introduction ... 7

Section 1 – Biblical Principles
Chapter 1: Giving God's way ... 13
Chapter 2: Living on gift income – a Biblical heritage ... 35

Section 2 – How and Why People Give
Chapter 3: Beginning your support-raising ... 63
Chapter 4: How do supporters decide to support you? ... 73
Chapter 5: Why do supporters decide to support you? ... 81
Chapter 6: Why we don't always feel comfortable raising support ... 95
Chapter 7: What can make potential supporters feel uncomfortable ... 109
Chapter 8: A few notes of caution ... 123
Chapter 9: Do your homework ... 129

Section 3 – Making it Work
Chapter 10: Getting going ... 137
Chapter 11: How many fish in your sea? ... 141
Chapter 12: Who tops your list? ... 145
Chapter 13: Get sorted ... 147
Chapter 14: Pepper mills and bridesmaids ... 151
Chapter 15: Taking the plunge ... 157
Chapter 16: The coffee-cup conversation ... 165

Chapter 17: "But it's not as simple as that for me…" 175
Chapter 18: Join the Scouts 181
Chapter 19: Postman Pat 189
Chapter 20: Show and tell 197
Chapter 21: Raising support from churches 205
Chapter 22: Meetings 219
Chapter 23: When the well runs dry 227
Chapter 24: Establishing a prayer team 239
Chapter 25: Keeping it going 241
Summary 248

Odds and ends

Funding your way through Bible College 253
Keeping your spiritual perspective 261
Useful contacts 273

So make yourself a hot drink, get a notebook and pen, and start reading…..

PREFACE

WHY I HAVE COME TO WRITE THIS BOOK

Much of this workbook stems from the experiences my wife Phyllis and I have had of raising support for over 30 years. I recognise that it therefore has a particular slant to it, a bias forged in the wonderful people we've met, the deep relationships we've enjoyed with our own supporters and the vital lessons we've learned over the years.

A giving heritage

I grew up in a Christian family who were heavily committed to mission. We were a basic Christian family, a bit above working class, living initially in the countryside on the outskirts of Strabane, in the west of Northern Ireland, and then in the town itself. My dad worked as an electrician with the local power company, eventually rising to become local district foreman. My mum looked after my older brother, myself and my younger sister as we grew up, only returning to work when my sister Ruth was in her teens. There wasn't a lot of spare cash around, especially in the early days, but it was a happy, stress-free life.

What made my parents stand out as different was their attitude to their possessions: they didn't have any. None at all. No home, no car, no food, not even any children. As far as they were concerned, they were looking after **God's** possessions. And they did it to the best of their ability, ensuring that everything God had entrusted to their care was used to the maximum impact for God's Kingdom. And that included us three children. As each of us came along, my parents committed us back to God to use however he wished for the sake of his Kingdom. They had enough sense not to tell us this and hang a sword of spiritual blackmail over our heads. They just waited to see what God would do and, sure enough, all three of us ended up in

Christian ministry. It was only then that we learned that they had expected us to make these choices all along.

But their giving wasn't just limited to their children. They kept from the income God provided them with only whatever was necessary for us as a family to live at a level they felt was right, and gave everything else away. Missionaries in far-off lands, people involved in Christian work locally, families facing hard times: they all felt the benefit of my parents' commitment to using the resources God had entrusted to show and tell God's love to those in need.

So I grew up not only as part of a giving family, but also as a gift to God myself, given by my parents. It still amazes me that God chooses to take us as a gift and then use us for his glory and for the extension of his Kingdom.

Learning to receive

It was December 1974 and it felt like running headlong into an emotional brick wall – yet I knew that it shouldn't feel like this.

Phyllis and I had just decided to join Agapé, then known as Campus Crusade for Christ. The decision itself hadn't been that difficult. We were young, starry-eyed and recently married, eager to do whatever God wanted us to do. It helped that my brother David and his wife Pam had been involved in Agapé from its inception in Ireland just a couple of years earlier, so we had some idea of what we were getting into. We'd supported them financially since just after we'd been married that February.

We were moving from Greenisland, outside Belfast, to Galway on the Irish west coast where we would be involved in student evangelism and also putting some administrative structure to Agapé's growing ministry. With both of us coming from office-based backgrounds, it seemed the best way to harness our professional skills and our Kingdom enthusiasm.

So, back to December 1974. My problem was that I was changing from being a giver to being primarily a receiver. I talked to others who raised support and they used terms like "we have to raise support too". In this context 'have to' is a negative term, with connotations of needing to undertake some unpleasant task. It isn't a term we use for something that's fun and enjoyable. This confused me. I knew from personal experience that giving is enjoyable. So where did the joy disappear between the giver and the receiver; what crack did it fall through?

To get the answers that would satisfy me, I decided to dig out all the passages I could find in the Bible about giving and receiving. As I explored the various passages on the subject, I was struck by a simple and obvious theme in what the scriptures say about giving and receiving – they always go hand in hand. **A giver can't give unless a receiver is prepared to receive and a receiver can't receive unless a giver is prepared to give.** JOHN 3:16 describes the ultimate gift from the ultimate giver, with us as the receivers. But even this fantastic gift of Jesus only has real impact in my life when I receive it.

And so it is with raising support. It is a partnership of equals – givers and receivers – each doing their part. After all, we are the family of God. For a family to function at its best, each member needs to play their part, using their gifts, personality and resources to make the whole family work as a unit. Each person is as important as the others – they just have different roles to play.

In God's family some are primarily **senders/givers** while others are primarily **goers/receivers**. Each is equal in his family. For you to be able to do what God asks of you as a goer/receiver, others need to do what God asks of them as senders/givers. **It's how God funds his family business.** You'll find other passages with this theme dotted throughout this book, especially in the first section.

When I realised that this was truly a partnership of equals within God's family, it caused two reactions in me. First of all, I wanted to ensure that our own personal giving was as sacrificial as it could be. While I may have been starting out on a road as a receiver, I knew that I could also play my part as a giver too. After all, Jesus said that it is more blessed to give than to receive [ACTS 20:35] so I didn't want those who were primarily givers to have all the fun! Secondly, I realised that by encouraging my friends to support us, I truly was introducing them to an involvement in God's family that they might have otherwise missed. It was as fulfilling for them to give as it was for us to receive, perhaps even more so.

This helped me see support-raising in a whole new light. It wasn't just about us getting the money we needed to do what God was calling us to do. **It was about God's children working together, each dependent on the other, to see God's plan fulfilled in the lives not only of the givers and receivers, but in the lives of those who were still outside the family.** What a privilege!

One of the exciting aspects of raising support, especially over the long term, is that what might start out as a simple support relationship with someone you might not even know, can lead to strong friendships and can bring benefits to all concerned, including the organisation you work for, that are way beyond what could have been envisaged at the outset. You cannot plan it, but you can watch closely to see how God develops relationships between his children in ways they didn't even suspect.

> *One of our early supporters was John, a young agricultural student who came to a summer Bible study conference we were helping organise. We clicked right from the start and he began supporting us, even when he was still a student. Not only did John support us himself, once he graduated and returned home to work on the family farm, he began introducing us to a number of his friends. One of these was Evan, who also became one of our supporters.*
>
> *Over the next few years we got to know Evan and eventually his new wife Clare quite well. They increased their support a couple of times, we ran an evangelism training course in their church, we went on holidays together, they helped organise an Agapé outreach project in their town. Again, it was one of those relationships that seemed to grow naturally.*
>
> *Eventually, Evan and Clare decided that they could use their gifts and experiences to help people in more need than those in Northern Ireland. Their contact with us made Agapé an obvious choice to explore, and they headed off to Malawi to work with the Agapé team there for some years before moving on to South Africa, where Evan's administrative abilities led to him taking on more and more responsibility. They eventually returned to the UK where Evan took on a senior role in Agapé UK, helping lead an organisation of over 100 staff working in a range of ministries in a range of countries.*
>
> *Although we left Agapé many years ago, we are still in regular contact with Evan and Clare and they still support us. More than that, Evan's and Clare's initial commitment, to support us as Agapé staff, eventually led to them having a major leadership role in the same organisation.*

Acknowledgements

The influence and input from many people over many years have made this book possible. If I were to express the appreciation I genuinely feel for each one, then this would end up as long as an acceptance speech at the Oscars!

However I want to pay a special tribute to my parents, Joe and Annie Wilson, who taught me how to receive from God and to give to others. They are both now in heaven enjoying the personal presence of the Lord and Saviour whom they faithfully served by being good stewards of the resources he entrusted to their care for their years on earth.

And to Phyllis, a true partner in all aspects of life and ministry, whose constant love and devotion to both God and to me is a delight and an encouragement.

Introduction

This workbook is for a special type of person. **If you are raising financial support from your own network of contacts to allow you to fulfil a call of God on your lives into some form of Christian ministry, then this book is for you.**

The way this call has been worked out in your life may well differ from the way it has been worked out in the life of someone else, even in the same organisation. God's word, the input of others, the direct prompting of the Holy Spirit to your spirit are all likely to have played a part in the formation and confirmation of your call. However you have come to know it, I'm using the term 'call of God' to mean a confidence that God is asking you to 'give up the day job', use your best working hours in direct Christian ministry and be funded by others to do so.

If you have read this far and you don't fit this category, then by all means, do read on. I hope you'll find something in the principles and practices outlined in the book that will help you in your own giving and receiving. But this book isn't really aimed specifically at you.

If you do fit the category, then you are very welcome. If you are just starting out on the exciting road of living by the financial support of others, I trust that this workbook will give you a lifetime of guidelines that you can build on using your own unique style. If you've been raising support for some time, I hope you will find some pointers here to a new direction for you, or perhaps just some confirmation of what you're already doing.

Before we start

I'm taking some factors as given in this book and won't be dealing with them in great detail. I'm assuming that:

- you do, genuinely, have a call of God on your life to do whatever it is that you are doing
- you have sorted out how your support will get to you in a tax-efficient way
- you or someone else has worked out how much you need to work and live effectively in the specific context in which God has placed you
- you have got good advice about your tax and employment status
- you've thought through your approach to life insurance, savings, pension, etc and you're comfortable with whatever conclusions you've come to
- you are immersing yourself in prayer during your support-raising. This isn't primarily a financial activity; it is spiritual ministry in the lives of you and your supporters and needs to be well protected in prayer.

If any of these are not the case, then you might need to do some work on them first, for this book to be of maximum benefit to you. Some of the references to other groups towards the end of the book should help with some of these issues.

What this workbook is about and how to use it

This is not a handbook of answers. In fact, as you work through it, it may well even prompt some questions you haven't already thought of. **What it is designed to do is to give you the confidence to answer your own questions for yourself.**

Raising support involves our hearts, heads and hands. We will be looking at all three in broad areas:

- Biblical principles of giving and receiving to engage the **heart**
- the whys and hows of giving to inform the **head**
- practical suggestions for raising support to equip the **hands**.

Experience has shown me that these three need to be dealt with in that order. So while I hope you work all the way through the book, if all you did was to explore the Biblical principles section and then put the book down, at least it would be a better start than simply rushing to the practical ideas section towards the end.

There are many stories scattered throughout the book, some about givers, some about receivers. They are all true, but in some cases I've changed some of the details to mask the identity of those involved. I'll leave it up to you to decide which stories have had details changed and which haven't!

p.39
How should I feel about raising support?

This is a workbook. **It is meant to be worked through, not just read.** Where there are parts for you to apply the material to your particular situation, please use them. There's plenty of scribble space all through the book as well as space to work on specific exercises. This is there for one purpose – to be used! However, if you'd prefer to keep the book in its pristine state, then I'd suggest that you buy a journal to use in parallel with the book as you work through it.

While there may be some key underlying principles that will help in your support-raising, there is no magic, one-size-fits-all formula. Raising support is a process of relationship-building and, as in the rest of life, any one set of support relationships will differ from another. This workbook will only be of real benefit to you if you make it your own, working out your plan in a way that suits your circumstances and your personality.

Non-ask or ask tradition?

It is worth noting at the outset that I grew up in a 'non-ask' tradition. In my home church it was viewed as being unspiritual and unbiblical to ask for money. This wasn't a concept that was necessarily shared by my family as I was growing up, but it did form part of my background.

I still recognise this stance as being a valid one, and one of the many ways that God chose throughout the scriptures as he provided for his people. It is, however, only one of the ways. Thankfully, in the scriptures we see God choosing to provide for his people using a wide spectrum of provision. This gives us quite a broad scope when we make our personal preferences in this area. I am an 'ask' person, a position I understand to be at least as equally valid as the 'non-ask' tradition of my background.

Over the years, Phyllis and I have personally seen God supply in a whole host of ways, including many times when I asked people and other times when I haven't. We've seen the timely miracle of the postman putting an envelope through the front door with a cheque in it for exactly the amount of rent we needed to pay the landlord who, just at that same moment, was knocking at the back door. We've also seen the equally miraculous regular monthly support that has allowed us to work to a regular budget for many years. Both are God's provision and need to be recognised as such, even if one seems more dramatic than the other. **God is the God of the ordinary in our lives as well as the God of the extraordinary.**

Throughout this book, I'm assuming that you have the freedom to ask people for support. However, all of the principles and many of the practices can be easily adapted if you choose not to. All I would ask is that you don't try to lock God into one philosophy or the other. He can, and will, choose to do what he pleases with your support, and it is likely to involve some mixture of provision, some of which will come through asking and some that turns up without you asking. **Just keep your heart in tune with God's and go with his flow.**

SECTION 1

BIBLICAL PRINCIPLES

CHAPTER 1

GIVING GOD'S WAY

It may sound obvious, but if you are going to receive financial support, someone needs to give it! And because you can't receive until they give, it is important to understand what the Bible says about being a giver before exploring what it means to be a receiver. Let's take a close look at some basic giving principles.

God is the ultimate giver

> *For God so loved the world that he gave his one and only Son, that whoever believes in him shall not perish but have eternal life.* [JOHN 3:16]

Try this sometime. Ask any group of Christians what is the best-known verse in the Bible about giving. In my experience, people usually suggest either *It is more blessed to give than to receive* [ACTS 20:35] or *Give, and it will be given to you* [LUKE 6:38]. A few keen Bible scholars might come up with some less well-known verses. But it usually takes a bit of prompting for somebody to come up with JOHN 3:16: *For God so loved the world that he **gave** his one and only Son, that whoever believes in him shall not perish but have eternal life.*

The best-known verse in the Bible about giving is the best-known verse in the Bible!

God is absolute in character. He gives because he is a giver and the cross is the ultimate gift, the act of supreme extravagance. God didn't try to find a cheaper alternative, or wait for a time when he would be able to pay less. He paid full price, giving his best, at great cost, for people who had done nothing to deserve the gift. In fact, they had shown by their actions that they deserved the very opposite of a generous, expensive and lavish gift. But, even in the face of rejection from those for whom the gift was intended, God still gave his son.

In creation, God made people in his own image and this would have included implanting in us his giving nature. But the Fall destroyed that, replacing God's giving nature with greed and self-centredness. When

Biblical Principles

we come into a faith relationship with God through Christ, God's spirit indwells us and he begins the process of building his character back into our lives. This should result in a growing understanding and practice of giving as God intended us to give.

But there is a constant battle between our old nature and God's spirit at work in us. This is seen as clearly in our use of money as in any other aspect of our lives. It was Billy Graham who said, *"A chequebook is a theological document. It shows who and what you worship"*. Jesus himself put it bluntly: *You cannot serve both God and Money* [MATTHEW 6:24].

In our societies money is treated by many as god and getting it is seen as the main aim in life. Meanwhile God is treated with apathy or contempt, and sacrificial giving is looked on as odd.

> *The husband of one of our long-time supporter couples has worked most of his life in a bank, rising through the ranks to a senior position with a very healthy income. Yet they live quite modestly, at a level way below their peers. Instead of simply tithing and giving ten per cent of their income to God's work, they sit down each year and work out what they feel, under God, they need for their own use. One hundred per cent of everything else is given away.*
>
> *One year his division had done particularly well and he got an unexpected, and significant, bonus. Because they had already worked out how much they needed that year, there was no discussion about how much they should give and how much they should keep – it was all given away.*
>
> *That is counter-culture. But it is an example of the practical reality of God's spirit working in the day-to-day lives of an ordinary Christian couple. This is not the kind of act of faith that is given a trumpet fanfare and has magazine articles and books written about it. But by quietly reflecting God's view of giving, this couple has had, and continues to have, a massive impact for the gospel throughout the world. Unheralded, but crucial.*

Point to Ponder

If God is the ultimate giver, and it is more blessed to give than to receive, what blessing does God receive by giving his son that is more than the blessings we gain as receivers of this ultimate gift?

What about you?

In the first place, we are receivers of the service of our Lord Jesus, who gave his life for us. [MARK 10:45]. Before we give or serve, we must acknowledge all that we have received from God and rejoice in it. How will this alter the way you live this week?

Verse

For God so loved the world that he **gave** his one and only Son, that whoever believes in him shall not perish but have eternal life. [JOHN 3:16]

Prayer – Use this prayer or write your own:

Father, I praise you for your lavish generosity to me and to all those in your family. What a gift: the sacrifice of the Son you love so much! I am needy and totally dependent on your mercy. You deserve my praise for such amazing grace. Amen

For further reflection

Read EPHESIANS 1:3-14 and revisit the 'Point to Ponder' on the previous page. What does God give us and what does he receive?

Giving God's way

It's all God's

Biblical Principles

Our societies are caught up in a mad rush to buy, own and upgrade as much as we can, as often as we can. Not only have we succumbed to compulsive consumerism, we even use it as a measure of success. Comments like, "He's done well" tend to be reserved for the person with the big car, the big house and the big bank account and not for the person with the good relationship with his wife and children, but who may never have had a well-paid job.

But what do we **really** own?

In 1 Chronicles we read of a very rich man who realised that he owned nothing. God tells King David that he wants a temple to be built as the focal point for the worship from his people. Because David has too much blood on his hands from a lifetime of battles and wars, God decides that it will be better that David's son, Solomon, builds it. All God asks David to do is raise the money!

David starts off the fundraising campaign by giving a very public major gift himself and then the other leaders follow with their gifts. When the rest of the people see how their leaders set the tone by their giving (*freely and wholeheartedly* [29:9]), they are delighted and eventually they give their time and abilities to add to the wealth given by the leaders to make the temple a reality.

When all the money is in, David calls everyone together for a prayer of consecration, praising God for his goodness and asking that the people's commitment to God be sustained. Right in the middle of his prayer David slips in what could almost be a parenthetical comment: *But who am I, and who are my people, that we should be able to give as generously as this? Everything comes from you, and we have given you only what comes from your hand.* [29:14] Even though David was the richest man in the kingdom and had given from what he referred to as *my resources* [29:2] and *my personal treasures* [29:3], he realised that, in reality, he owned nothing. **All that he and the others had done was to give back to God what God had given to them to look after in the first place.**

Do you remember the first time as a child you bought your parents a gift? Perhaps it was Christmas, a birthday or Mothering Sunday. If you were like me, you probably took your pocket money and splurged out on something tacky and inappropriate, wrapped it up with as much sticky tape as paper and presented it proudly. How did your mum or

> *But who am I, and who are my people, that we should be able to give as generously as this? Everything comes from you, and we have given you only what comes from your hand.*
>
> [1 Chronicles 29:14]

dad react? Usually, of course, parents are delighted. Not because of the gift itself (would she ever use that perfume? would he ever wear that tie?), but because their child has chosen to use some of their pocket money to buy a gift for them. But where did the child get the pocket money? From the parents! All the child has done is use some of the money they were given by their parents to buy a gift to give back to them. In spite of the child's pride at their giving, it is the person to whom they have given the gift who has made it possible for the gift to be bought.

> **Point to Ponder**
>
> Imagine (and write down) how you would feel if a child of yours (real or imaginary) refused to use any of the money you gave him/her to buy you a present.

Our giving to God is just like this. No matter how much we give to God, it has all come from him in the first place. While we may mature as Christians, we never really are anything more than dependent children, only returning to God the time, abilities and money he has chosen to give us.

Biblical Principles

What about you?

Sometimes parents may not respond to gifts from their children with joy. But our Father God delights in our giving back to him. As a child of God, what could you change this week in your attitude to giving?

Verse

Everything comes from you, and we have given you only what comes from your hand. [1 CHRONICLES 29:14]

Prayer – use this prayer or write your own:

(Perhaps you could rewrite the above verse as a prayer of thanks.)
Father, thank you that you have given me so much. Thank you that I am able and willing to give back to you and so be a partner in your work in the world. Thank you that I can be generous because of your greater generosity. Amen

For further reflection

List the people you have met and the possessions you have used in the last 24 hours (or the last week, or longer if you wish).

Read COLOSSIANS 1:15-16. Spend time pondering the wonder of the fact that all these people and things in your list were made by God and for God. Respond with praise.

God wants everything used for the extension of his Kingdom

Too often our agenda in life bears little resemblance to God's agenda. As God himself said: *For my thoughts are not your thoughts, neither are your ways my ways* [ISAIAH 55:8]. This divergence of priorities is seen most clearly in how we use money. And it's not just a modern issue; it was an issue for people in Jesus' time too. So much so that Jesus deals extensively with the subject of people's fascination with material well-being in the Sermon on the Mount. For example: *Do not store up for yourselves treasures on earth, where moth and rust destroy, and where thieves break in and steal. But store up for yourselves treasures in heaven, where moth and rust do not destroy and where thieves do not break in and steal* [MATTHEW 6:19-21].

Not much has changed in 2,000 years. At its heart, our life's agenda is still dominated by accumulating things that rust, can be stolen and get eaten by moths.

But God's agenda is about the extension of his Kingdom. That's the whole point of the cross – providing a way for people to switch from Satan's kingdom to God's Kingdom, while satisfying God's justice that the penalty for being in Satan's kingdom was paid.

If God entrusts resources to us, and his priority is the extension of his Kingdom, then we should assume that he wants us to use these resources for his benefit, not simply for ours.

My parents were an unspectacular couple, with a spectacular impact for God's Kingdom. The whole focus of their lives was to use everything they had in the best way they could to ensure that people heard, saw and felt the love of God. For example, when we were children they told us that when they died we would not inherit the family home; it was to be used for the benefit of missionaries. Following my dad's death in 1995, my mum continued to live in the home and in the spring of 2005 the three of us children discussed with my mum how this desire could best be achieved when the time came. We had researched various options, and in the end my mum was very happy with the plan to sell the house and give the funds to places overseas that provide hospitality to missionaries. Just a few months later my mum died quite unexpectedly and, in the midst of our grief at our sudden loss, we had the joy of cashing in her only asset of any significance and giving away all of the money.

Also following her death, I got a form from the tax office to complete so that my mum's tax file could be closed and whatever tax she had paid since the beginning of the tax year could be repaid. It was a typical tax form and would have taken me most of a day to find out all the information they needed. I really didn't have the time or emotional energy to spend on this, so I did a quick check and realised that almost all of the tax my mum had paid that year had already been reclaimed through Gift Aid by the various charities she supported. There was only £7 left. And that was because she was careful to let the causes she supported claim tax back on only a percentage of what she gave them so that the total tax being reclaimed wouldn't be more than she actually paid!

I phoned the tax office and explained this, asking if I needed to complete the form if there was only £7 to be repaid. The person at the other end of the phone asked me to clarify this. Did I mean that my mother had given away virtually all of her taxable income? I assured him that she'd given away a lot more than her taxable income, but Gift Aid had only been reclaimed on part of her giving. He'd never come across this situation before and it took a bit of convincing before he realised that I had the figures right. "Your mother must have been quite a giver," he said. "There's no need to fill in the form. I'll deem the file to be closed."

My parents were like everyone else in God's Kingdom: sinners whose sins had been forgiven. But they had realised early on in their married life that they were receivers. They had received everything they had from God and none of it belonged to them. It was then just a logical step to want to make sure that they maximised these resources for the rightful owner. It wasn't their agenda that counted; it was God's.

Point to Ponder

What, in **your** life, would you be **un**willing to give up even if it was absolutely necessary in order for you to keep in step with **God's** agenda?

▶▶ (For example, favourite hobbies, regular job promotions, half your money, your respectability, your current church family, your parents' support, your competence and skills, your home, your children's education, your job, your spouse's support, all your money and possessions, your own life,…)

What about you?

A Christian pastor admitted to a youthful prank where he broke into a shop and changed all the price tags around, so that the cheap things now had expensive price tags and the expensive things had cheap price tags. This is what a worldly agenda does to what God values. Jot down now two or three ways that you will try to work hard to see the true value of everything. (Remember that our culture all around us is weakening our willingness to value things as God does.)

Verse

...store up for yourselves treasures in heaven, where moth and rust do not destroy and where thieves do not break in and steal. [Matthew 6:20]

Prayer – Use this prayer or write your own:

Our loving provider-God, I treasure you as all that I truly need. Thank you for those you have raised up to support me financially and pastorally because they treasure you and your eternal agenda more than their own material comforts. Bless them today with lives that treasure you even more. Amen

For further reflection

Read John 17:1-5.
Notice that Jesus' agenda is his Father's glory and his own glory. How did he achieve this? Remember what is just about to happen Jesus.

Read Matthew 6:19-24
Our hearts are very easily led away from true treasure in heaven, when we treasure anything that is not God's. Use the list of things you would be unwilling to give up that you wrote in the 'point to ponder' on the previous page and do the following:

- Spend time in your heart and mind treasuring those things that will last for ever and rejoicing over them. Think of ways that you can show your love and devotion to God in the coming week.

- Spend time in your heart and mind putting non-eternal things in their proper place. Think of ways that you can prevent non-eternal, material things from stealing your devotion from God.

Biblical Principles

Everything is lent to us to look after

An occupational hazard of cross-cultural mission is temporary homelessness. Whether you are waiting to move overseas, are back for a few months in the middle of some years abroad, or have finally returned home after living and working in another land, you'll do well if you get through it all without a bit of a panic from time to time about where you'll unpack the suitcases and rest your weary head. It has happened to us more times than I care to remember, and we're so grateful to family and friends who made beds available to us when we needed them. One family of supporters have even had us stay with them on three different occasions – now that is a supporter worth having!

On one occasion, when we were moving to Agapé's European office in Germany, we sold our home in Northern Ireland much quicker than we had planned and needed somewhere to live for a few months. Around the same time we met Ian and Roberta Clarke who themselves were preparing to go to Uganda to set up what became Kiwoko Hospital. They needed someone to house-sit for a few months while Ian completed a tropical medicine course in Liverpool. Their home was just what we needed, just when we needed it.

It was a beautiful home, right by the sea, with a large upstairs lounge overlooking the bay for long summer days and a small cosy downstairs lounge with a log grate for long winter nights. In addition to being a doctor, Ian had been a partner in a pine furniture business, so we even slept in a pine four-poster bed! It was a fantastic home to live in, even for just a few weeks. But it wasn't ours; it was simply entrusted to us to look after for a short time. And that had an impact on how we treated it. We were much more careful with their home and its contents than we would have been had they been our own.

One day we accidentally burned one of their saucepans beyond the point where a brillo pad and some elbow grease could restore it to its former glory. If it had been our own, we would have simply picked up some cheap replacement somewhere. We knew that Ian and Roberta wouldn't mind. But we minded. It wasn't ours, it was theirs and we had ruined it. We ended up looking everywhere

> *trying to find a replacement as close as possible to the original so that we could leave the home as we had found it.*
>
> *It was a genuine privilege to live in that home and we really enjoyed it. But we were looking after it on behalf of the owners and that adds a sense of responsibility to the privilege. Even as I write this, I'm spending a week tucked up in a friend's holiday home on the Donegal coast, catching up on lost writing time and, again, being careful with a home entrusted to our care for a time.*

So, how do we treat the resources God has entrusted to our care? Right at the outset, by giving man an overseeing role in creation, God set the standard: *Be fruitful and increase in number; fill the earth and subdue it. Rule over the fish of the sea and the birds of the air and over every living creature that moves on the ground.* [GENESIS 1:28]. God is the owner; we are simply his agents. He expects us to care for everything he commits to us, maximising his resources for his Kingdom, while allowing us to benefit as well.

We haven't always done a good job, whether on a global scale or a more local scale. But even if you can't play a leading role in the major environmental and conservation issues of our day, how are you doing looking after the time, abilities and money that God has entrusted to you? Do you recognise God's ownership of them? If someone else watched how you use them, would they conclude that you were working towards God's agenda of extending his Kingdom, or an agenda of your own?

The constant battle between our old, sinful nature and God's spirit makes this a daily challenge, no less so for those who have committed their lives to working full-time in Christian ministry.

When my father died we wanted to chisel a verse on his tombstone that we felt reflected his life. We chose 1 CORINTHIANS 4:2, using the King James version, which said it best: *It is required in a steward that a man be found faithful.* **God asks us to do no more than to faithfully look after what he entrusts to us.**

Point to Ponder

Be honest with yourself and God: do you truly recognise God's ownership of your time, abilities and money? What do you use at present as if it is yours and not God's?

Biblical Principles

What about you?

How might you transform each of the items on the list you made in the previous section (page 20) so that they are cherished and used fully for God's purposes, not just your own?

Choose the item you are most hesitant to give up and hand it/him/her over to God's care and love.

Verse

Whoever can be trusted with very little can also be trusted with much, and whoever is dishonest with very little will also be dishonest with much. So if you have not been trustworthy in handling worldly wealth, who will trust you with true riches? And if you have not been trustworthy with someone else's property, who will give you property of your own? [LUKE 16:10-12]

Prayer – use this prayer or write your own:

Father, thank you for giving me access to your riches as your partner in your work. Please help me to be faithful as I seek to use all that you've lent me to bring you glory. Amen

For further reflection

Read LUKE 19:1-27
Jesus came into the life of Zacchaeus and changed him from a selfish accumulator of wealth for himself into a generous steward of God's wealth. Jesus came to rescue such lost people [v.10]. How has Jesus coming into your life changed your attitude to wealth and integrity?

Jesus is **not** like the hard man of noble birth [vs.12, 21]. There is nothing that Christ "did not put in", so he is fully justified in expecting us to look after properly what he has given us. Looking after the gifts of our King is **not at all** like looking after a beautiful painting by locking it up in a vault [v. 23]. He expects us to put all that he has entrusted to us "to work… until [he] comes back" [v. 13]. Reflect on Christ's return and how this truth will help you to work better with all that God has entrusted to you: with each of your possessions, your family members, your work, and with each ability and spiritual gift.

Reflect on the fact that the more we put what God has given us into his eternal work, the more he entrusts to us [vs. 24-26]. [See also LUKE 16:9-15]

Give from what God has, not from what you think you have

Paul's relationship with the church in Corinth was, to say the least, prickly. A substantial part of his letters to the church is spent correcting, advising and instructing on issues as diverse as incest, legal actions between Christians and disruptive worship practices. On a number of occasions Paul also tackles the way the church gave, or, more to the point, did not give. In 1 CORINTHIANS 9 he deals with their decision not to support Paul himself, returning to this theme in 2 CORINTHIANS 11 and 12. Later in the book we will look at Paul's issues with the Corinthians in relation to his personal support from them.

In 2 CORINTHIANS 8 and 9, Paul deals with the way the church failed to follow through on a commitment they had made to give a gift to help the church in Jerusalem, which was quite poor and suffering from food shortages, probably as a result of a famine. The Corinthians were the first to sign up to this appeal and were also the first to actually start giving. But then, after having started so well, they stopped.

> See 1 CORINTHIANS 16:1-4; ACTS 24:17; ACTS 11:29-30

In these two chapters, with a combination of threats, encouragement, coercion and persuasion, Paul urges them to complete the gift that they had agreed to give. It appears that the Corinthians felt that they could not afford to complete their pledge. In today's terms, they had checked the church budget, realised that they didn't have enough coming in to meet their committed outgoings, so had to cut back on some of their giving. Paul encourages them to recognise that their commitment was a call of God. It wasn't limited by their bank balance, but only by their ability to trust God to supply what they needed to fulfil what he had called them to do, while also supplying for their own needs.

> *And God is able to make all grace abound to you, so that in all things at all times, having all that you need, you will abound in every good work.*
> [2 CORINTHIANS 9:8]

There is an important lesson here. Sometimes God asks us to give of our time, abilities or money in a way that seems illogical and beyond our visible means. It may seem that we simply cannot afford it or are not properly equipped for it. **But God has limitless resources and he will always equip and resource us for what he calls us to do, even when we have no idea where the resources will come from.**

Take Peter, for example. Peter and the other disciples are in a boat, crossing the Sea of Galilee in the middle of a storm [MATTHEW 14:22-32]. They see what they think is a ghost walking on the water near them and, not surprisingly, they are terrified. But, of course, it isn't a ghost, it is Jesus and he calls out to them telling them not to be afraid. Peter, reacting with characteristic impetuosity, calls back: *Lord, if it's you, tell me to come to you on the water.* Jesus says *Come.* So Peter throws his leg over the edge of the boat and walks on water. We are not told how far he got before he started to wobble and Jesus had to stretch out and grab him but as far as I know, it was a lot further than anyone else has ever managed!

Peter did what Jesus asked him to do – and against all the odds he succeeded. He didn't try out his water-walking skills at the shallow end of the swimming pool. He didn't head to the nearest Christian bookshop to buy the latest water-walking book or sign up for the seminar. He simply acted on what Jesus said and it worked. He may not have been one hundred per cent successful, but he got far enough for Jesus to stretch out his hand and grab him.

What about us?

When God asks us to do something, often our first instinct is to look at our own resources and then determine whether or not we can do what he is asking us to do. We may end up giving from the visible and limited resources we think we have rather than from the sometimes invisible but always limitless resources God knows that he has.

Maybe it's because we are often better at talking to God than listening to him that we don't hear his voice, directing us. Maybe it's because we enjoy giving in a way that satisfies our own emotions, needs and desires that we block out God's direction to us. We need to learn to recognise God's voice in the midst of all the other voices clamouring for our attention, act on what he asks of us and believe that he will provide whatever we need to complete what he calls us to. And this is true for people living on gift income too, worried they will never raise enough support. **It all starts with a spiritual ear tuned in to God's voice.**

Giving God's way

Jeremy and Clare were quite well off, with Jeremy's job in the city paying a good six-figure salary. But this was all about to change with them choosing to leave their secure financial lifestyle and join a UK-based Christian ministry. Not only did it mean a 75 per cent reduction in their income, they would also be responsible for raising all the support needed for both their salary and all their ministry expenses. It was a big step for a couple who had been so self-sufficient for so long.

For some years Jeremy and Clare had arranged for all their giving to go through Stewardship and at the outset of this major change in their life and lifestyle, they made a commitment to continue giving as much as they could.

The months rolled by and Jeremy and Clare's support got stuck at around 70 per cent. Suddenly Jeremy realised that, although they were channelling their giving through Stewardship, they had forgotten to tell Stewardship where the money should be given on to. He checked; their Stewardship account had £6,000 in it!

Quickly he rationalised the situation – this money was to be given to Christian causes; they had given most of it when they were still in 'normal' jobs; surely it would be OK for them to use this money for their own ministry. Then he stood back and looked at what he'd just thought. No, this money was not to be used for themselves, even if it would be used for Christian ministry purposes; it was to be given away.

So, right at the time when they most needed money themselves, they instructed Stewardship to give away the whole £6,000.

The next week they got a £12,000 gift from a new supporter.

> **Point to Ponder**
>
> Check your daily priorities, making sure that you set aside enough time every day to hear God's voice from the Bible.
>
> ▶▶ How does this time compare with the amount and quality of time you spend listening to other voices, e.g. TV, friends, colleagues, books, films, …? God is our all-sufficient guide. Trust him with your life direction. [PSALM 119:9,11; PROVERBS 3:5-6; ROMANS 12:1-2]

Biblical Principles

What about you?

God has limitless resources. How much money do you need to fund the mission activity you believe God wants you to do? How much have you received so far? How much have you given away so far?

Decide now the amount of your first year's income that you will give away, and choose the people or missions to give it to. If you have already raised this much, consider giving it away now… but only if you will do it cheerfully! [2 CORINTHIANS 9:7]

Verse

And God is able to make all grace abound to you, so that in all things at all times, having all that you need, you will abound in every good work. [2 CORINTHIANS 9:8]

Prayer – use this prayer or write your own:

Father, please remind me daily of your limitless resources. By your Spirit, give me the courage I need to trust you to provide everything at the right time for the work you would have me do for your glory. Amen

For further reflection

Read LUKE 21:1-4

The rich put more notes and coins into the temple treasury than the poor widow, yet Jesus is clear that, in God's economy, the widow "put in more than all the others". If the widow had thought in worldly terms, she could have concluded that her two meagre coins would make no difference at all to the needs of the temple and that she would be better off keeping them and living a little longer [v4]. So what do you think this demonstrates about the attitude towards God of the poor widow? [See also 2 CORINTHIANS 8:1-5]

God's way of giving includes the promise of a return

There are many differences of opinion about what is often termed 'Prosperity Gospel'. At its extreme, it is the sort of teaching that says if you give £10 to God he'll give you £100 back and it is most critically typified by the worst excesses of American tele-evangelists.

But is it actually true that if, as an example, I give £10 to God that he will give me £100 back? Well, it is and it isn't. Look at what Paul says to the Corinthians. We need to remember that Paul is encouraging the Corinthians to fulfil their giving commitment. He uses a range of arguments and persuasions to get them to understand the importance of giving: *Whoever sows sparingly will also reap sparingly, and whoever sows generously will also reap generously… Now he who supplies seed to the sower and bread for food will also increase your store of seed and will enlarge the harvest of your righteousness. You will be made rich in every way so that you can be generous on every occasion, and through us your generosity will result in thanksgiving.* [2 CORINTHIANS 9:6, 10+11]

Clearly, Paul is saying here that when the Corinthians give they will be made rich, and not only in financial terms, rich in every way! This certainly sounds like the £10/£100 argument. But look at why they will be made rich – it is so that they can give even more away. **So you can be generous on every occasion.**

As we give, we get, so that we can give more, and get more, so that we can give more… This is an example of the principle outlined by Jesus in the parable of the talents in MATTHEW 25:21: *Well done, good and faithful servant. You have been faithful with a few things; I will put you in charge of many things.* **As we show ourselves faithful in using the money God entrusts to us, then he will give us more, so that we can be faithful in even more.**

Biblical Principles

> A few years ago, a girl in her early 20s in my parents' church decided to join a Christian organisation where the staff raise their support. Ever keen to encourage young people into Christian ministry, my parents offered to support her. They were then in their 70s and had little spare cash, with all three of their own children living on support, so the girl assumed that they couldn't really afford to support her. For several weeks she didn't give them the necessary forms to complete, despite a number of reminders.
>
> Eventually she handed over the forms, which my dad gave back to her the following week, duly completed. Still unsure if they really meant it, the girl said that she'd hold on to the forms for a couple of weeks in case they changed their minds. My dad didn't often get annoyed, but this reluctance to take their support really got to him. "Why are you trying to stop God blessing me?" he almost shouted at her!
>
> Later that week he got a letter from his company pension scheme unusually announcing a mid-year increase in his pension. The next Sunday he showed the girl the letter, saying, "See what you almost stopped me getting!" Then they put the extra pension amount into the church building fund.

It was Larry O'Nan, a friend who has taught and written about stewardship for decades, and from whom I've learned a huge amount, who coined the term **God's Authorised Wealth Distributor** to describe someone who recognises and practises God's principles of stewardship, using their resources under God's direction for the sake of his Kingdom. But long before I heard Larry's term *God's Authorised Wealth Distributors*, I'd seen it in action in my parents. As a child you may also have had role models among your family or older friends who exemplify a Godly understanding of giving. If not, then you can begin the process in your generation and begin being a role model for the generation coming on behind you.

But a word of caution. If we think that we are on to a good thing and stop the process at the 'getting' part of the cycle, we cease to be faithful and God will look elsewhere for his Authorised Wealth Distributors.

"What is the smallest percentage of my income I can give and still be a generous giver?" What's wrong with this question?

What about you?

At the moment, how much of your regular income do you give away to gospel ministry? Would you say that you are being generous? Could you trust God to increase this over the next few years?

Write a plan to increase the proportion of the wealth God will entrust to you that you will invest in the eternal work of his family. For example, this year x%, next year add 1% or 2%, 3rd year add another 1% or 2%, ... 10th year aim to be giving y% – whatever you decide cheerfully to give.

Verse

Remember this: Whoever sows sparingly will also reap sparingly, and whoever sows generously will also reap generously. [2 CORINTHIANS 9:6]

Prayer – use this prayer or write your own:

Father, please bring a great harvest of righteousness and generosity into the lives of those who give to support my ministry. May they know your blessing in every area of their lives. Amen

For further reflection

Read 2 CORINTHIANS 9:6-15. Apart from money, how does this principle apply to our time and abilities, our family and career, etc?

Has anyone ever said to you, "Thank you – every little helps" when you have given them a gift? How does this comment show that the receiver is not thinking about you as the giver?

When the poor widow in LUKE 21 gave of herself (see page 28), she may not have received huge monetary rewards, but the harvest of her generosity was her growing righteousness [2 CORINTHIANS 9:10]. What a difference if the receiver, instead of saying "Every little helps" had said, "Thank you. The Lord knows all our circumstances and he will bless you for this".

Biblical Principles

God wants his children to give cheerfully

> *Each man should give what he has decided in his heart to give, not reluctantly or under compulsion, for God loves a cheerful giver.*
> [2 CORINTHIANS 9:7]

My knowledge of Greek isn't great. But one of the few words I do know is the word translated as 'cheerful' in 2 CORINTHIANS 9:7. *Each man should give what he has decided in his heart to give, not reluctantly or under compulsion, for God loves a **cheerful** giver.*

So what exactly does it mean to be a **cheerful** giver? The Greek word here is *hilaros* and is the same root word from which we get the word hilarious. God loves hilarious givers!

Paul has just told the Corinthians that they need to complete their promised gift, that he will come and collect it and that he will send some men in advance to make sure it's ready. He even says that he might just bring some Macedonians along with him (who, in contrast to the Corinthians, had completed their gift even though they were a poorer church), thereby threatening the Corinthians with acute embarrassment if their gift isn't ready. And then he says that he doesn't want them to feel pressured into giving, but that they should be giving 'hilariously'! I wonder what the Corinthians made of all this?

Paul is getting at a basic principle here: **the need of the church in Corinth to give outweighed the need of the church in Jerusalem to receive**. In fact, nowhere in these two chapters does Paul say what the gift is needed for – no stories of starving children, no pleading on behalf of those much worse off than themselves. Paul emphasises that giving, in and of itself, is important. It shouldn't be done reluctantly, nor under compulsion, but out of the sheer joy of knowing that God has asked us to do something that will bring benefit to his Kingdom. That, in itself, should give us all the satisfaction and buzz we need.

But too often we settle for much less and we get our buzz by satisfying our own emotions through our giving. We might even be giving to the right cause, but not with the right motivation. Again, it comes down to listening to God's guidance, doing what he asks us to do and being absolutely delighted that God has trusted us to be part of his plan. What could be more *hilaros* than that?

Point to Ponder

Do **you** find it a joy to be involved in God's purposes through giving to a friend doing mission somewhere out of your personal reach? What has convinced **you** to give so cheerfully?

What about you?

Often we are reluctant to ask people to become financial partners in our ministry because we worry that they will be reluctant to give or will feel compelled to give if we ask. How can you counter that reluctance on your part to ask?

Verse

Each man should give what he has decided in his heart to give, not reluctantly or under compulsion, for God loves a cheerful giver. [2 CORINTHIANS 9:7]

Prayer – use this prayer or write your own:

Father, it is such a joy to be a partner in your work at the other side of the world or among different people groups at home by giving to someone in gospel ministry. Thank you for those who give cheerfully to my ministry. Amen

For further reflection

Read Revelation chapter 5 – or even better, take time to read the whole book. Try to sense what it will feel like to be there when God is finally seeing the fulfilment of his eternal purposes for his creation. What a massive excitement. What a spectacular demonstration of power. Today, right now, God allows how we use the gifts of our money, time and abilities to play a part in this tremendous plan.

This should make our giving all the moare hilaros. His purposes are wonderful beyond words; eternal priorities that far surpass this dying world's priorities. Amazingly, God works with us to fulfil his purposes in our generation. There is no greater joy in life than knowing that we are working together with others in God's family to see his wonderful purposes fulfilled all over the place through our life and giving.

How can you help others in God's family grasp these things, and understand and become excited by the vision God has given you to be part of his purposes?

Biblical Principles

SUMMARY

- Give with generosity
- Give your best
- Give with the needs of others in mind
- Give with a spirit of thankfulness and praise
- Give in a way that your resources will be multiplied
- Give with expectancy
- Give now, not later

Notes

CHAPTER 2

LIVING ON GIFT INCOME – A BIBLICAL HERITAGE

In the previous chapter we looked at some of the Biblical principles that should underpin our **giving**. I suspect few of your supporters, whether individuals or even churches, will have spent a long time working out their theology of giving. Most people support you because they know you, like you and think that what you are doing is worthwhile. But it is important for you, at least, to have a grasp of the Biblical basis of what they are doing.

In this chapter we will take a look at the **receiving** side of things. When I started out raising support, this was often called 'living by faith'. But that's not a term I'm comfortable with, because of the implications. Paul tells the Romans that *everything that does not come from faith is sin* [ROMANS 14:23]. Does this mean that if those who raise support live by faith, then those whose income comes from a so-called 'normal' job live lives of sin? I guess not.

Anyway, it takes much less faith these days to live on a support basis that it does to have a 'normal' income. Most of your supporters have only one source of income: their employer. In these days of short-term contracts and limited job security, all it takes is too much red ink on the balance sheet and the job's gone. But, by raising support, you have many sources of income. If one of them has to drop off for whatever reason, you will still carry on with the bulk of your support and be able to replace the supporter who has stopped – and probably much more quickly than someone who has lost their only source of income will be able to find another job. If anybody lives by faith these days, it's the supporters!

Biblical Principles

Trading income – gift income

There are two basic forms of income: **trading** income and **gift** income. With trading income, you give someone money and they give you goods or a service in return. So for example, you go into a restaurant and give them £20; they give you a meal. With gift income, you give someone money for them to provide goods or a service for a third party. So, if you give the same £20 to Tear Fund, World Vision or Christian Aid, you don't expect them to arrive at your door with a meal. You expect them to use your gift to feed someone else.

Throughout history, God has set apart specific people to be involved in his ministry and to live by gift income. Because God has asked them to spend their normal working time working for him, using a whole range of ways to show and tell his love to people in need, they don't have time to generate a trading income by working for someone else. They need to be supported by others who have an income.

The scriptures give us a number of examples of people who lived by the support of others as they served God full-time. Here are three key examples and in the rest of this chapter we will look at each in turn:

- The Levites
- Jesus and the disciples
- Paul

The Levites

Then the Lord said to Aaron, "You will have no inheritance in their land, nor will you have any share among them; I am your share and your inheritance among the Israelites. I give to the Levites all the tithes in Israel as their inheritance in return for the work they do while serving at the Tent of Meeting".
[NUMBERS 18:20-21; read the whole passage 18:8-32]

The Israelites had been in Egypt for around 400 years. Although they were made welcome initially and given the best land to live on, things went downhill in later years. Eventually they ended up working as slaves for the Egyptians. After God's dramatic intervention through the plagues, and under Moses' leadership, the Israelites had the chance to escape from Egypt and return home to Canaan quite quickly. But their fear of the people who occupied their homeland outweighed their faith in God, so they spent another 40 years wandering around the desert on the fringes of Canaan – so near, but yet so far.

During this time in the desert, God began preparing them for what would eventually become a settled life back home in Canaan. They had been away from their homeland for so long, without their normal social structures around them, that they needed to re-learn how to live normal life again. It would be as if everyone in Britain had gone to France in the early 1600s, only returning today. No one would have any idea about what British society, culture and tradition should look like.

Funding the Levites

In this passage in Numbers, God is setting in place the funding structures for the Levites – the people who worked full-time for God in those days. Being an agriculturally-based economy, income was linked to land. However, God told Aaron that the Levites wouldn't get any land when they returned to Canaan. No land meant no income, so how would they survive? Given all the risks that the Levites had taken on this tortuous journey through the desert, and the way they had acted as intermediaries between God and the people and vice versa, this decision didn't seem fair.

But if God had given land to the Levites, what would they have done with it? When would they have found time to work it? It would have been no use to them. They were already spending their working days directly serving God in the tabernacle. Having land would have been a distraction. Something would have suffered: either their farms or the work God had called them to.

To get round this dilemma, God introduced the first structured financial support system. It is the system that has formed the basis since then for everyone called to work full-time for God. Even those who work for organisations where they get paid from general funds also live on a support basis. In most cases, the income into these general funds still comes through gifts from God's people. The difference is that there is no direct link between the givers and the receivers.

God's solution was to get the rest of his people to set aside some of their income (tithes) to give to the Levites, so that they could concentrate on their work for him. Notice that God uses the term 'inheritance' three times in these two verses in Numbers when outlining how the Levites would be funded. In our society we tend to associate the word inheritance with something we receive from a relative who has died. But the Hebrew culture had a more far-sighted view of generations than we have. Just think of the number of times terms like 'to the children's children' are used in the Old Testament. To them the concept of inheritance was more one of a constant flow, from one generation to the next.

The Hebrew word used here for inheritance, *nachalah*, is the same word used for a stream or brook flowing through a valley. It conveys the idea of something that connects two sides. In this case, it connected the giving of the Children of Israel through their tithes with the receiving of the Levites, as they spent their days working directly in the cause of God's Kingdom. And a stream keeps flowing, constantly wending its way through the land for as long as it takes to reach the sea.

God's inheritance

God is well able to provide an instant fix for an immediate need. But he also shows his interest and concern for us over the long term, building sustainability and even taking account of the generations following on behind us. God is as interested in our future, and the future of our children, as he is in the present. And, just as with the Levites all those thousands of years ago; today his inheritance, or stream of our support, continues to be the connecting point between the givers and the receivers.

Even though the Levites abused this system of funding from time to time, adding to it through their own black economy that insisted that the people used only animals sold by them for sacrifices, the underlying principle was established.

Our world is very different from the early days of the return of the Israelites to Canaan, and we can't transplant the exact practices from this context and drop them into 21st century mission work.

But we can say that it has always been God's idea, right from the outset of structured ministry, that those unable to have a job that brings them an income because they work full-time in his Kingdom should be funded by the rest of his people.

Point to Ponder

How do you think the Levites would have felt when God told them that they were not going to receive any land to get an income from or as an inheritance, but were to live now and for the generations to come on the gifts of others?

- uncomfortable?
- frightened?
- it's not fair?
- excited?
- privileged?
- other …?

What about you?

How do you feel about living on the gifts of others?
- uncomfortable?
- frightened?
- it's not fair?
- excited?
- privileged?
- other ...?

If your answer was one of the first three listed, then remember that the rest of the Israelites were to give support to the Levites as part of their worship of the God who provided for them. This is still true today: you receive your income as part of God's people's worship of him.

How does this make you feel?

If your answer was one of the last two listed, then remember that the Levites were not chosen by God to minister full-time and live on the gifts of others because they were more spiritual or more gifted than the rest of the Israelites. It is an exciting privilege to be supported in God's work by the gifts of others, but it is never a cause for arrogance or spiritual superiority.

How does this make you feel?

Verse

Whatever you do, work at it with all your heart, as working for the Lord, not for men, since you know that you will receive an inheritance from the Lord as a reward. [COLOSSIANS 3:23-24]

Prayer – use this prayer or write your own:

Father, I admit that I'm *uncomfortable* (or whatever other emotion fits you) with the prospect of raising support and living on the gifts of others. Thank you that it isn't a new thing, but it has always been your chosen way to fund your mission in the world. Please help me to become excited by sharing in this privilege. Amen

For further reflection

If you are living on the gifts of others, is it wrong to save some of this money for your pension, or for your children? Look at 1 TIMOTHY 5:8. How does this influence your decision about saving for your family's future needs?

The Levites were not exempt from offering to God the best of what they received from the rest of God's people [NUMBERS 18:25-32]. Receivers are still to be givers too.

Jesus and the disciples

Biblical Principles

After this, Jesus travelled about from one town and village to another, proclaiming the good news of the Kingdom of God. The Twelve were with him, and also some women who had been cured of evil spirits and diseases: Mary (called Magdalene) from whom seven demons had come out; Joanna the wife of Chuza, the manager of Herod's household; Susanna; and many others. These women were helping to support them out of their own means.
[LUKE 8:1-3]

At the outset of his ministry, just after his baptism, Satan tempted Jesus to turn stones into bread – to use the gifts and abilities that were readily available to him to provide for himself. Jesus' response is well known and often quoted: *Man does not live on bread alone* [LUKE 4:4]. Jesus' ministry was not about performing tricks to satisfy his hunger and the curiosity of a fickle public. His strength did not just come from the food he ate: it also came from his relationship with God his father. And his father's business was not about to be compromised just because Jesus was hungry.

But this still left a question. How would he provide for himself and his growing band of followers? He had encouraged them to leave their normal jobs and follow him. If he wasn't going to use his miraculous powers to provide for them, what exactly **was** he going to do?

If you and I had been asked to put together a funding plan for the ministry of the Messiah and his disciples, what would we have come up with? Perhaps we would have contacted Godly, wealthy businessmen and encouraged them to give a gift. We might even have suggested to Jesus that he reconsider his decision not to go down the miraculous route. Think of the added benefit of showing people that he really was the Messiah. Perhaps we would have recommended that some of the disciples work a couple of days each week at their former jobs. With this part-time income, and some gifts from friends, there might be enough to keep everyone going.

But what option did Jesus choose?

Jesus chose to fund his ministry through the gifts of committed friends

The people who supported Jesus had had their lives affected by Jesus prior to supporting him. They were not trying to pay for the spiritual benefit they had received. They were just expressing their thankfulness in a way that they could.

You will find that the best and most committed supporters will include those with whom you have some sort of spiritual or ministry history. Perhaps it is someone who had an important influence in your life as a young Christian, or someone in whose life you have had an impact. It could be someone you have been involved with in leading some church activity, summer camp or short-term mission project. Of course, not everyone who supports you will have some sort of spiritual or ministry history in your life, but they are a good group to start off with in your quest to see who God has set apart to support you.

Those identified in this passage are all women and at least some of them had questionable reputations. Take Mary Magdalene, for example. Some traditions say that she had been a prostitute – maybe she was, maybe she wasn't, we don't know. Another of those listed, Joanna, was the wife of Chuza, who was a major figure in a political process well known for its corruption. Their family income was therefore almost certainly tainted. What's more, her husband's boss's predecessor had been the King Herod who had tried to kill Jesus as a baby. Now Jesus helps to fund his ministry from resources that most likely originated from this Herod's treasury!

This was a high-risk approach.

Jesus was not known for choosing the safe option. By choosing to be supported by Mary, Joanna, Susanna and the others, Jesus demonstrates supreme humility. All things had been created by him and for him [COLOSSIANS 1:16]. Yet here we see the creator of the universe in human form, choosing to be financially dependent on people created by him, some of whom might have even felt out of place in our churches today!

Did he need their money? Clearly not. He didn't **need** to receive gifts from anyone. He could have provided for himself and his disciples miraculously – he showed this in the feeding of the five thousand.

But Mary, Joanna, Susanna and the other supporters needed to give. In a society dominated by men, with legalistic religious rulers determining who was and who was not acceptable to God, where else could women like Mary and Joanna have found a fulfilling involvement in a life of faith? Their lives had been radically changed by their encounter with Christ and now they wanted to help proclaim the message of the Kingdom. For Mary Magdalene, with all the social and religious exclusion that her previous lifestyle would have brought, getting up in the morning knowing that she was helping fund the Messiah must have brought a huge sense of fulfilment. And where else in that society could Mary and Joanna have shared a common commitment and involvement? It was only in their new-found faith that they had common ground, and a key way they expressed their faith was through their financial support for Jesus.

Supporters come from all backgrounds

Whatever the social structures of Jesus' time, it is clear that Mary and Joanna came from opposite ends of the spectrum, with Jesus probably somewhere in the middle. In the normal course of life, none of these three would have been drawn together.

While your supporters, at least initially, will come mostly from your own network of friends, you are also likely to have supporters from well beyond your social experience. Some will be people whom you would not have expected to support you. You may not know them that well. You probably wouldn't choose to go on holiday with them. They might be much poorer than you and you'll feel guilty taking their money. They might be much richer than you and you may be intimidated by them. But, for whatever reason, some people whom you wouldn't automatically choose to be on your support team **will** sign up. And it will be more to do with God fulfilling a need in their lives than with him fulfilling a need in your bank balance. **Remember, they need to give to you much more than you need to receive their support.**

I was asked by a mission agency to lead a two-day support seminar for their staff and also to spend time with their director looking at his support situation in particular and the mission's overall communication in general.

In all, I was with the director for four full days and was amazed at the breadth of his contacts. As well as a good group of peers, he had contacts who were socially both below him and well above him. During the few days I was able to meet some of his contacts, including a number who were Christians in senior positions in the business community. While he was happy enough to receive support from some of his contacts, he told me that he felt intimidated by the wealth and position of those whom he considered to be above him socially and was reluctant to approach them for support either for himself or for the mission. He hoped

> they would somehow recognise his need for support and give it, without him having to take any initiative. Even then he said he would feel uncomfortable being supported by people of such standing in the business community.
>
> However, in chatting with a couple of his business contacts they commented how much they were in awe of him! What they saw in the mission director was someone whose education and training would have ensured a career with a very good income, but who had chosen a path that would have much more eternal impact than their jobs would ever have. And why did they not support him? He had never asked them, so they assumed his needs were being met from somewhere else.

What about 'funny money'?

Whether or not Mary's money came from a previous life of prostitution is debatable. However, Joanna's would almost certainly have come from the corrupt political system that funded Herod's household. The source of the money seems to have been less important to Jesus than the heart-motivation of the giver. Remember that all the wealth in the world ultimately belongs to God, so there is no such thing as ungodly money, just God's money in the hands of ungodly people. It is unlikely that you will be offered financial support that weighs heavily on your conscience. But, if you are, what do you do?

The Corinthian church faced a similar problem [1 CORINTHIANS 8]. They didn't know if it was right to eat meat that had been offered to idols. To summarise Paul's response to this issue, he said that it was just meat. Being offered to idols hadn't changed it and it was no problem to eat it.

Unless…! If eating the meat caused the Christians in Corinth to sin or caused someone else to sin, then eating it became a sin.

You should use the same rule of thumb for any money that you are offered that you know to be in some way suspect. It is still God's money, and so you are free to take it.

Unless…! If by taking the money it causes you or someone else (including the person offering you the money) to sin, then you shouldn't take it. So if it feels to you that you are condoning or even colluding with the way in which the money has been obtained – or that others will assume you are – and if that makes you feel uncomfortable, look elsewhere for your support.

Biblical Principles

> *During a support training session, one of the new staff of the mission involved announced that he would have nothing to do with lottery money. A few months later he phoned me at home one Sunday afternoon. At church that morning he had been approached by a couple who had recently become Christians and were beginning to question whether they should continue gambling on the lottery. The previous week they had won a small amount and knew that if they kept it they would only be tempted to keep spending money on lottery tickets. They asked if the missionary would take the money and use it for his work. If he took it, they said, it would help them stop buying lottery tickets.*
>
> *What did he do? He took the money!*

I do not quote this story to illustrate the rights or wrongs of the lottery, but rather to show that God's agenda in our support-raising is not always the same as ours. In this case the couple's need to give was connected to their spiritual growth as young Christians. Frankly, receiving the small amount of money involved did not make any real impression on the large amount the missionary family needed to go halfway round the world. But giving the same amount met an important need in the lives of the couple who gave it.

It is important to be careful about pre-judging your potential supporters and thereby possibly ruling out the equivalents of Mary and Joanna in your life. Remember, there is no such thing as Christian money and non-Christian money, only God's money. **Sometimes he chooses to do unusual things with his wealth, and through unusual people.**

> *The earth is the Lord's, and everything in it.* [PSALM 24:1]

If it was good enough for Jesus, it's good enough for us

Jesus not only expressed humility by choosing to live by the support of ordinary people whose lives had been turned round in an extraordinary way through their commitment to him, he modelled it too. He has also left us an example to aspire to. **Living by the gifts of others isn't a step down in the economic pecking order of life. It's a step up; it's a calling to live the same way Jesus did.** God doesn't offer that privilege to many people, and some who are offered the option turn it down because they cannot cope with being dependent on others. God's family is interdependent. If God is calling you to live by the gifts of others, it isn't just about you getting money from others, it is about the supporters' lives being fulfilled as they give to you. Jesus knew that, and if it was good enough for him, then it's good enough for you and me.

Point to Ponder

In the story about the mission director who didn't ask his many rich friends to support him, how do you think his friends felt when they discovered that he **did** need their support but had never asked them?

What about you?

Maybe living on gift income feels like a step down in the economic pecking order for you. Is it a shock to realise that this is the way the creator and owner of the world, our Lord Jesus, chose to live when he was here? When you feel bad about it, remember that there is a man in heaven who knows what it feels like and who approves of living this way. And thank him.

God's economy is so different from a worldly one. How do you feel about the idea that other people need to give to you much more than you need to receive their support?

Verse

Peter said to him, "We have left all we had to follow you!" "I tell you the truth," Jesus said to them, "no one who has left home or wife or brothers or parents or children for the sake of the Kingdom of God will fail to receive many times as much in this age and, in the age to come, eternal life." [LUKE 18:28-29]

Prayer – use this prayer or write your own:

Father, thank you for the humility of Jesus, being prepared to live by the gifts of his friends to allow him to complete the work you had called him to. Please empower me by your Spirit as I seek to follow his example and live by the gifts of my friends as I seek to fulfil the work you have called me to. Amen

For further reflection

How would you feel if someone who had been notorious (eg, made money from internet porn or drug dealing) turned to Christ in prison and became one of your major financial partners, and this became known?

Biblical Principles

Paul

Paul was the original pioneering missionary. After his dramatic conversion he abandoned his former life of persecuting Christians and became an energetic missionary to the Gentiles in what was still, primarily, a Jewish church.

He travelled tirelessly all around the northern Mediterranean for years, preaching the gospel and planting churches. But his success came at a cost. His own account of what he endured during his missionary journeys makes uncomfortable reading – beatings, floggings, imprisonment, hunger, shipwreck, stoning [2 CORINTHIANS 11]. Not only did Paul endure all sorts of physical and emotional hardship during his years in mission work, he also had varying degrees of success in developing a financial support team to fund his work.

In this section we'll look at possible reasons why the Corinthians (who knew him well) didn't support Paul; why the Philippians (who hardly knew him at all) did; and why Antioch (his sending church) didn't support him financially during a critical phase of his ministry.

Paul and the Corinthians: where it didn't work

[Read 1 CORINTHIANS 9:1-14; 2 CORINTHIANS 11:7-9; 12:11-20]

This is my defence to those who sit in judgement on me. Don't we have the right to food and drink? Don't we have the right to take a believing wife along with us, as do the other apostles and the Lord's brothers and Cephas? Or is it only I and Barnabas who must work for a living?
Who serves as a soldier at his own expense? Who plants a vineyard and does not eat of its grapes? Who tends a flock and does not drink of the milk?
Do I say this merely from a human point of view? Doesn't the Law say the same thing? For it is written in the Law of Moses, "Do not muzzle an ox while it is treading out the grain." Is it about oxen that God is concerned? Surely he says this for us, doesn't he? Yes, this was written for us, because when the ploughman ploughs and the thresher threshes, they ought to do so in the hope of sharing in the harvest. If we have sown spiritual seed among you, is it too much if we reap a material harvest from you?
If others have this right of support from you, shouldn't we have it all the more? [1 CORINTHIANS. 9:3-12]

Sometimes people you had fully expected to support you choose not to do so. Their reasons may seem illogical to you. You might even be a bit hurt by their decision. But at least you are in good company, as this example from Paul's experiences of living on gift income shows.

Paul had a strange relationship with the church in Corinth. He had stayed there for 18 months towards the end of his second missionary journey [see Acts 18:1-11], most probably also visiting them again for a short time during his third journey.

By the time Paul is writing to them, the church appears to have become well established, if somewhat wayward and confused. In his letters, Paul deals with some issues about which they had asked for his input. He also takes them to task on a few points of his own, especially where he has become aware of problem areas in the church.

One issue Paul had with the church was their lack of financial support for his own ministry. He argues that he had the right to expect them to support him, but that he didn't exercise this right because they were not mature enough to cope with it. He explains that, although he chose to work to earn his own living, he should not have had to do so, commenting, *The Lord has commanded that those who preach the gospel should receive their living from the gospel* [1 Corinthians 9:14].

Another letter from Paul...

In his second letter to the Corinthians, Paul again takes them to task for not being mature enough to accept their responsibility to support him. With a mixture of annoyance and sarcasm, he says, *Was it a sin for me to lower myself in order to elevate you by preaching the gospel of God to you free of charge? I robbed other churches by receiving support from them so as to serve you. And when I was with you and needed something, I was not a burden to anyone, for the brothers who came from Macedonia supplied what I needed. I have kept myself from being a burden to you in any way, and will continue to do so* [2 Corinthians 11:7-9].

And in 2 Corinthians 12:11-13 he writes, *I have made a fool of myself, but you drove me to it. I ought to have been commended by you, for I am not in the least inferior to the 'super-apostles', even though I am nothing. The things that mark an apostle – signs, wonders and miracles – were done among you with great perseverance. How were you inferior to the other churches, except that I was never a burden to you? Forgive me this wrong!*

Again, Paul emphasises that he had the right to have been supported by the Corinthians, but chose not to, accepting support from others instead. He even stresses that his position as an apostle, which they appeared to question, was enough justification for them to have recognised their responsibility to support him. But, as in his first letter, he says that he has no intention of asking them for financial support because he does not want to put at risk either their spiritual development or his relationship with them.

But, if he isn't going to ask the Corinthians for support because it might damage them, why go to all the trouble of explaining this to them? Why not just let it sit as one of the 'what ifs' of his ministry? Surely the very act of taking them to task for not supporting him, in itself, ran the risk of damaging them and also his relationship with them?

This was the first century church. They didn't have 20 centuries of church history to look back on. They didn't have the completed scriptures that form the bedrock of informing our faith and practice. They were struggling to work out how much of the Jewish and other cultural traditions that accompanied the early Christians, including even Paul, should be incorporated into church life. They were also dealing with people from hedonistic, idol-worshipping backgrounds. No one had given them the *How to Support Your Missionary* manual. Apparently they were supporting some people [see 1 Corinthians 9:12], but they hadn't sorted out their criteria for support. Paul argues that he, above all people, should have been supported by them.

By helping them understand **why** they should have supported him, embarrassing as the process might have been for the Corinthians, it was setting a platform for future missionaries and Christian workers raising support. **And you and I still benefit from his comments to this day.**

But why did the Corinthians not support Paul?

After all that he had done for them, and the selfless way he had worked on their behalf, you would have expected them to be at the front of the queue offering to support Paul. But they weren't even in the queue at all. Even worse, it appears from this passage in 1 Corinthians 9 that they had made a conscious decision not to support Paul. Is it any wonder that he was seriously miffed by this?

This may well be a chicken and egg situation. Did they choose not to support Paul because of what they viewed to be his attitude towards them, with Paul arguing in these passages that even if they had offered support, he wouldn't have taken it? Or did they offer support with strings attached and Paul refused it? It may have been that some people in the Corinthian church wanted to control Paul by applying their support in the form of patronage, a practice not uncommon for teachers in that society. The problem would have been that the patron would have expected the teacher to teach what they wanted to hear – and Paul was the last person to agree to be controlled by his supporters.

Whatever the reason, it is clear that the Corinthian church had questions about Paul's style of ministry: they questioned whether he was really an apostle; thought his teaching was too harsh; and had a low opinion of him as a speaker. By focusing on the style of Paul's ministry, they lost sight of the man in the centre of the ministry. So they chose not to support him, in spite of all he'd done for them.

This messy situation left Paul clearly disappointed and hurt. **It also meant the Corinthians losing out on a blessing that they should, and could, have had.**

> Tom and Sue are originally from the US but have worked with an evangelism ministry with Muslims in Europe for many years. Shortly after the attacks on the World Trade Center and the Pentagon in September 2001, they returned to the US for a few weeks to visit their supporters. They were astounded to be contacted by two different supporters who told them that they were so angry at the Muslim community that they were stopping Tom and Sue's support because they worked with Muslims! It didn't make sense. Because of their anger at Muslims, they were stopping support for a Christian couple – and a Christian couple who were working to bring Muslims to Christ!
>
> Tom and Sue got to meet one of these supporters personally. He, somewhat reluctantly, accepted that their ministry was important and agreed to continue their support. They could only manage to speak to the other supporter on the phone. He was so bitter in his response to the attacks on his country that he refused to budge and cancelled his support.

Sometimes issues about the style or nature of your ministry can determine whether or not a supporter will give. They can be issues that are important to the giver but to the receiver might seem illogical, irrelevant or downright ridiculous. But when something that is important to the giver gets in the way of them seeing the receiver as a person, then you can end up with a response like the one that faced Tom and Sue. To you, the response of the giver (or potential giver) might seem daft, unreasonable or simply wrong. But to them it makes sense.

By all means, try to work out the differences, especially if there are clear misunderstandings involved. But there may be times when you will need to walk away, recognising that there are irreconcilable differences that are going to be too much trouble to try to overcome. Don't be negative or judgemental about anyone who chooses not to support you over an issue about which you disagree. Pray a blessing into their lives and pray that they will find some other aspect of God's Kingdom that they can support cheerfully and with enthusiasm.

> **Point to Ponder**
>
> Imagine you are a wealthier member of the Corinthian church and have been a patron of several good public speakers before you turned to Christ, paying them well and expecting them to say what you wanted to hear. How would you feel about Paul's attitude to preaching [1 CORINTHIANS 9:11-23]?

What about you?

Can you think of a situation in your ministry where a supporting church (or major financial partner) has tried, or might try, to 'force' you to do something different from what you believe God wants you to do? How did/would you feel about this? If a close Christian friend, or a significant church you've been a part of, decides not to be a financial partner with you, then you are in good company (eg, with the apostle Paul). Write down the way you would respond to this situation:

- for your relationship with God and the mission work he has set you apart to do
- for your ongoing relationship with your friend or church.

Discuss this with a respected leader in your church or mission agency.

Verse

Do not judge, and you will not be judged. Do not condemn, and you will not be condemned. Forgive, and you will be forgiven. Give, and it will be given to you. A good measure, pressed down, shaken together and running over, will be poured into your lap. For with the measure you use, it will be measured to you. [LUKE 6:37-38]

Prayer – use this prayer or write your own:

Father, thank you that you are my provider, not my supporters. I acknowledge that your choice of supporter for me is always the best, even when I would have chosen differently. Help me to see your hand in both the disappointments and the encouragements. Amen

For further reflection

Sometimes we try to second-guess the responses of our partner churches, and then are tempted to write letters to justify their support for us based on what we think they want to hear. How do you feel about finding yourself in this situation?

Though understandable from a human perspective, gospel ministry is God's work and our integrity is key. However we feel, we mustn't lose the truth on the way.

Biblical Principles

Paul and the Philippians: where it did work

Yet it was good of you to share in my troubles. Moreover, as you Philippians know, in the early days of your acquaintance with the gospel, when I set out from Macedonia, not one church shared with me in respect to giving and receiving, except you only; for even when I was in Thessalonica, you sent me aid again and again when I was in need.

[PHILIPPIANS 4:14-16]

Paul's relationship with the Philippians was very different from his relationship with the Corinthians. However, in some ways it was equally strange. From what we read in ACTS 16, Paul was in Philippi for a relatively short time – probably just a few weeks and certainly much less than the 18 months he spent in Corinth.

Apparently a few people had become Christians, including a girl who earned money as a fortune-teller. One impact of her new-found faith was that she gave up her fortune-telling, much to the annoyance of her bosses who lost a valuable source of income from her work. When they made an official complaint, Paul and Silas were arrested and imprisoned, only to have an earthquake hit the prison that night. The prison governor rushed in, afraid that he'd lost all his prisoners. Not only did he find that all the prisoners were still there, he also found faith in Christ, and he and his family were baptised in the middle of the night. Then next morning Paul was released, left town and headed towards Thessalonica and the rest of Macedonia. He was back for a brief visit during his next missionary journey, catching a ship in Philippi on his way to Troas. [ACTS 20:6]

By the time Paul was writing his letter to the church at Philippi, he was under house arrest in Rome, towards the end of his life, with few people he could preach to. (Once he'd shared the gospel with all the prison guards, who else was there?)

What prompted Paul to write this letter was a gift that he had been sent by the Philippians, brought by Epaphroditus, who had been taken ill after arriving in Rome. The Philippians had heard about this and were concerned. To show that Epaphroditus had fully recovered, Paul sent him back to Philippi carrying his thank-you letter for the gift. **Essentially, Philippians is the first recorded letter from a missionary to his supporters.**

Although the Philippians hardly knew Paul, it appears that they considered themselves to be an important part of his support team right from the outset:

In all my prayers for all of you, I always pray with joy because of your partnership in the gospel from the first day until now. [1:4-5]

It is also clear that they have supported him financially over a period of time, that the support wasn't just a one-off gift and that they had started supporting him right after he had left them for Thessalonica. It also seems that they had stopped supporting him, and this gift was them starting up again [4:10, 15-16].

Credit where credit's due

There was obviously a strong connection between the Philippians and Paul. Unlike his letter to the Corinthians, the tone of this letter is warm and friendly, with very little corrective comment. Paul reminds them that they are living in a crooked and depraved generation in which he says they shine like stars in the universe [2:15]. What a beautiful way to describe supporters! He is also much more self-disclosing in this letter, even going as far as telling them that he thinks it might be time for him to die. He debates with himself in the letter whether it would be better to die and go to be with Christ, or stay alive a while longer so that he might do more work and get to see the Philippians again. His choice? To postpone going to be with Jesus so that he might get to visit his supporters again! [1:21-26]

In terms of their support for him, he tells them twice that he doesn't really need their money [4:11, 17] but that he is still pleased to receive it. This isn't a self-deprecating false modesty. He really didn't need their money: he was under house arrest – what could he spend it on? **But he knows that it is important that they give, whether or not he needs to receive.**

He tells them that their account has been credited by their giving [4:17]. The word 'credited' here isn't a technical term associated with double-entry book keeping, but rather it is a statement reflecting benefit to them as they gave.

But how can their account be credited by their giving? This comment only makes sense when we realise that supporting someone isn't about money. **It is about the supporter playing their part in God's eternal plan for his Kingdom, and this participation brings credit with it in God's books.** The money bit should simply be the financial expression of a heart commitment. Not all supporters know this. In fact, Paul thought it important to remind the Philippians of the importance, to them as well as to him, of their support.

In our church life we have had well over a century of holding up the receivers as the being the most important in the process, so diluting the reality that **the givers and receivers are all members of God's family, each equally important in the role they play**. If one or the other family members do not play their role, then the Kingdom of God suffers.

He also tells them that their needs will be met [4:19]. This verse is very often misapplied to missionaries and others who live on a support basis. While it is true that God looks after those he calls to work directly in Christian ministry, that isn't what this verse is about. This promise is for the **supporter**, not the person being supported. Those receiving support can only claim this in so far as they support someone else.

Remember that Paul was hardly known by the Philippians, especially compared with how well he would have been known by the Corinthians. Yet they were still supporting him towards the end of his life, when he was in prison and not sure if he should even keep living!

It is clear that their relationship with Paul wasn't based on his current effectiveness, nor even on a long-standing close friendship. It was based on a spiritual connection that God brought into being. The Corinthians were so concerned about peripheral issues surrounding Paul's ministry that they lost sight of the man in the middle of it all and didn't give the support that logically they should have given. The Philippians, despite hardly knowing Paul and despite the limited effectiveness of his ministry at this time in his life, willingly supported him.

> **Point to Ponder**
>
> As people give money to gospel ministry, their 'bank account' in heaven goes up not down. As you think about receiving money from your friends and partners, how does this truth improve how you feel?

What about you?

List the people and churches who have given to you so far. Rejoice in the Lord that they have received this blessing from him.

One year you receive 50% more income than you need. Do you:
- write to the givers thanking them but telling them to stop, or reduce, the amount they are giving?
- write to the givers thanking them, thank God for blessing them more and prayerfully consider whether to give the extra money to other ministries you support or to find new ways to spend the extra money God has provided for your ministry,
- do a combination of these?

Write down the reasons for your answer.

Verse

And my God will meet all your needs according to his glorious riches in Christ Jesus. [PHILIPPIANS 4:19]

Prayer – pray this prayer for your individual financial partners:

Father, you love to bless your children. I praise you for all the blessing you pour out on those who give generously. From your glorious riches in Christ, please meet the every need of (name of financial partner). Amen

For further reflection

Read PHILIPPIANS 1:20-26; 4:10-20. Paul writes to his supporters saying he is delighted with the gift he has received, even though he isn't sure he will live long enough to spend it, and anyway he doesn't need it. How would you feel about expressing such things in a letter back to your supporting churches and partners? How can you learn from Paul's attitude to these things?

Biblical Principles

Paul and Antioch: did the home church drop the ball?

In the church at Antioch there were prophets and teachers: Barnabas, Simeon called Niger, Lucius of Cyrene, Manaen (who had been brought up with Herod the tetrarch) and Saul. While they were worshipping the Lord and fasting, the Holy Spirit said, 'Set apart for me Barnabas and Saul for the work to which I have called them.' So after they had fasted and prayed, they placed their hands on them and sent them off. [ACTS 13:1-3]

Some time later Paul said to Barnabas, "Let us go back and visit the brothers in all the towns where we preached the word of the Lord and see how they are doing." Barnabas wanted to take John, also called Mark, with them, but Paul did not think it wise to take him, because he had deserted them in Pamphylia and had not continued with them in the work. They had such a sharp disagreement that they parted company. Barnabas took Mark and sailed for Cyprus, but Paul chose Silas and left, commended by the brothers to the grace of the Lord. He went through Syria and Cilicia, strengthening the churches. [ACTS 15:36-41]

Moreover, as you Philippians know, in the early days of your acquaintance with the gospel, when I set out from Macedonia, not one church shared with me in the matter of giving and receiving, except you only.
[PHILIPPIANS 4:15]

What a send-off into mission work Barnabas and Saul (as Paul was still known at the time) got from the church at Antioch. Church leaders worshipping and fasting, the Holy Spirit speaking, more fasting (this time with prayer), hands laid on Barnabas and Saul, and off they went. No doubt about their call!

But the 'dream team' of first century mission didn't last long. As happens too often in Christian ministry, there was a serious relationship breakdown between the two men. Barnabas, with his encouraging and pastoral heart, wanted to give Mark a second chance, especially as they were cousins! Paul, with his focused pioneering spirit, wasn't having it. Mark had had his chance and blew it. Paul wanted somebody more reliable. So they split up, heading in different directions with different team members: Barnabas gave Mark his second chance and Paul got his Mr Reliable in Silas.

As we saw in the previous section, a few years later Paul was writing to the church in Philippi referring back to the time he left the Macedonia area and reminding the Philippians that they were his only supporters at that time. But what about Antioch? Didn't they send money to Paul? Well, apparently not, at least during the time that Paul is referring to in his letter to the Philippians. So what had happened to their support? Why was the fanfare of the send-off not matched with ongoing and continuing financial support?

The simple answer is that we don't know. But let's explore a couple of possibilities.

Getting money to Paul wasn't as easy as it is for our supporters to get money to us today. There were no standing orders or cheques. Paul's supporters had to collect the money, get somebody trustworthy to carry it and hope that Paul was still where they thought he was by the time the money arrived. So maybe it was simply a matter of logistics that the Antioch support didn't get to Paul at that stage in his ministry.

Or maybe Paul got caught up in early church politics. Barnabas was the key leader in Antioch before Paul arrived. In fact, it was Barnabas who brought Paul to Antioch [ACTS 11:22-26]. Their disagreement brought an abrupt end to what had been a good working relationship. Thankfully it appears that Paul was reconciled to both Barnabas and Mark later in his life. But is it possible that some time after the bust-up between the two men, Antioch sided with Barnabas? We've already looked at one church who should have supported Paul but didn't (Corinth). Maybe it happened with Antioch also.

Whatever the reason, we know that for at least part of his missionary life, the church that sent Paul on his way didn't follow this up with financial support. But God ensured that the support that was missing from Corinth and Antioch, financially as well as spiritually and emotionally, was more than made up for by the Philippians, even though Paul hardly knew them compared with the other two churches.

When people choose not to support you

So, if you find yourself with a church or individual who chooses not to support you, even when they may have seemed enthusiastic about your work initially, don't despair. **God will provide other supporters**, maybe even people you hardly know at the outset, but who, like the Philippians with Paul, will go on to become committed friends.

A word of caution. It isn't comfortable to have someone decide not to support you. It is even less comfortable when someone who has been supporting you for some time decides to stop. In most cases their decision to stop is due to changes in their financial circumstances, or a change in their interests. In a few cases it might be because of something in your work that concerns them – a new direction in your ministry, a lack of communication with them, some activity you've got involved in that they disagree with, or whatever. In these situations it is important to remember that you are accountable to God for your ministry, not to your supporters. They, like us, are brothers and sisters in God's family and we work in partnership with them.

Biblical Principles

Point to Ponder

Sometimes even your original sending church may choose to stop financing you. This does not mean that your mission work must end.

However, it is always worth listening to what they have to say about your work, even if you might not agree with their comments. We should approach any possible difference of opinion with supporters with an open mind, recognising that God might be using them to speak to us about some aspect of our lives and work.

SUMMARY

The tradition of some of God's people being set apart from direct income-generating work and being supported by others is a heritage founded in scripture and carried on throughout the life of the church. It didn't always work smoothly in the examples we find in the scriptures, but it has always been God's idea. We are privileged to follow in this tradition.

What about you?

Whether or not the church in Antioch chose to stop financing Paul, sometimes key supporters do decide to stop their support. What would happen if some of your key supporters who were very keen at the start decided to stop supporting you? Could you thank God for them?

Verse

Bear with each other and forgive whatever grievances you may have against one another. Forgive as the Lord forgave you. [COLOSSIANS 3:13]

Prayer – use this prayer or write your own:

Our Father, we may well feel snubbed by those who have been our friends and partners in your work. They may have acted carelessly or even sinfully. Forgive us when our responses are simply protecting our own pride. Forgive them when they have neglected your good name or brought your work into disrepute. Please bless them greatly as they put their resources and energy cheerfully into other work for your Kingdom. And give us an increasingly generous heart. Amen

Notes

Biblical Principles

SECTION 2

HOW AND WHY
PEOPLE GIVE

CHAPTER 3

BEGINNING YOUR SUPPORT-RAISING

We've looked at some Biblical principles of giving and of receiving. We've looked at the Biblical heritage of being supported by God's people. But how does all this work out in practice? What goes on in the mind of a supporter, or potential supporter, as they consider supporting you? What goes on in our mind as we face the reality of being supported by others? What needs to be in place for someone to be able to make an informed decision about supporting you?

First of all, you need to recognise that each supporter will support you for a mixture of reasons. Helping meet your financial need is just one of the reasons, and your need for support will, of course, **trigger** their decision. But your financial need is not, in itself, their primary motivation. Meeting needs of theirs (consciously or subconsciously) will be a major factor in their decision to support you.

In this section we will explore some of the hows and whys of all this, looking at motivations, comfort zones, striking the right balance between **informing** and **asking** and other bits and pieces that make raising support such an adventure:

- How supporters decide to support you
- Why they choose to support you
- Why we don't always feel comfortable raising support
- Why potential supporters can feel uncomfortable
- Homework to do before you start planning how to raise support

Before we consider these, however, it is worth looking at some of the basic starting points about how you view supporters and the process of support-raising.

Supporters are already there

Has your decision to work in Christian ministry caught God by surprise? It may be a surprise to some of your family and friends. It might even have come as a surprise to you. But God was well aware of it long before you even thought of it. **His call on our lives always pre-dates our awareness of it.**

If you are working with a Christian organisation or mission agency, something connected to that organisation will probably have played some part in helping awaken God's call in your life. It might have been a speaker, website, magazine, brochure or maybe someone you know who worked with the organisation. Then the application process will have helped test this call to ensure that you will cope with the rigours of whatever is ahead of you.

If you are working independently, I assume that you became aware of a need somewhere and are following God's call to address that need, having tested the validity of the call with your church and others. Again, God's call was already there on your life and he used questions and answers, some asked by you and some by others, to bring his call to the surface at the right time.

If God has gone to all this trouble to ensure that you have heard his call on your life to give your time to some task in the cause of his Kingdom, do you think that he has a similar call on those who will give their money to the same task? **Remember, this is God getting his family to work together, the givers and receivers working in partnership. As a loving father, he doesn't want any member of his family to have their life unfulfilled. That is as true for your supporters in their giving as it is for you in your receiving.**

You don't have to invent, create or make supporters…

… God has already done that. **All you need to do is discover where they are.** In some cases they may not yet be aware of God's call on their lives to support you. In the same way that there has been a process to awaken God's call on your life to give your time to the work he has called you to, there needs to be a process to awaken the call of God on their lives to give their money.

See pages 25–26.

We saw earlier that God enables givers to give what he asks them to give. **God will not put a call in your supporters' lives to give without also putting his call in your life to receive.** Similarly, he will not lead you into Christian ministry without providing those whose giving will make his call in your life a reality. That doesn't mean it will be easy. In fact, discovering who out there has been prepared by God to join your support team may take you a lot longer than you think. But there is enough money. It's just a case of getting it into the right bank accounts!

Don't depend on distant miracles

Every few weeks I get a call or email from somebody raising support who wants to know if I can give them a list of trusts who would fund them. I usually phrase my reply in a way that aims to get the person to ask different questions. Questions that help them focus on contacts closer to home than some distant trusts where they have no relationship.

Raising support isn't just about getting the money you need. It is about exploring the relationships God has already given you to see who he has called to be part of your support team through their finances, prayers and encouragement. ☞ **Start at the centre of your existing relationships and work out. Don't start at the outside and try to move in.**

Would you give regular financial support to someone you didn't know, had never heard of and who wasn't introduced to you by anyone you know, just because they asked you for money? You might give a pound to someone shaking a collecting box in the street, but you're not likely to sign up for significant monthly support for a totally unknown person. Trustees of trusts are no different. They want to make sure that the money entrusted to them has the maximum impact to meet the needs that the trust was set up to meet. They are much more likely to give to people and projects they know and trust than to someone they've never heard of, no matter how worthy your cause seems to you.

Chasing distant miracles can result in you spending precious time and emotional energy with little or no response. Time and emotional energy that would be much better used sitting down with your friends, over a cup of coffee, sharing what God has put on your heart and asking if they'd like to be part of it. Not only are you much more likely to get regular financial support, you're also much more likely to get consistent prayers.

Your real goal isn't financial

As you raise support, you probably have some sort of target that you're working towards. This may have been set for you by the organisation you work with or, if you work independently, you must have some sort of amount in mind that you think is what you need to work and live at an effective level.

Yes, you do need to make sure that you have enough money to do what God is calling you to do. There are no extra spiritual bonus points for living on the minimum all the time. In fact, some of the most materialistic people I know are missionaries on low support. So much of their time, prayers and energy are focused on the next meal, the next bill, the next everything. Their lives become so focused on money, and their lack of it, that they fall into all the money traps Jesus warns about in the Sermon on the Mount.

But your real goal isn't about raising money. **Your real goal is to raise up people and create solid, long-term partnerships.** If, for example, one person offers to provide all your financial support for as long as you need it, you will have hit your financial target, but you will have too narrow a support base. For your spiritual protection and personal encouragement you need the heart commitment of a sizeable group of people. Given that Jesus said that the heart follows the treasure, the best way to secure the heart commitment of enough people is to get their treasure in the form of financial support. Although it isn't absolutely true in all cases, Phyllis and I have found that those who support us financially are more interested in our work and more committed to us than those who have chosen not to support us. Similarly, we tend to take a keener interest in those we support financially than those we don't.

For where your treasure is, there your heart will be also.
[MATTHEW 6:21]

You already have all the skills you need

Support-raising isn't a science of getting the formula right; it's an art of building relationships. It's not about how well designed your support leaflets are nor how heart-tugging your cause is. **It's about being able to express what God has put on your heart in as personal a way as possible to those he has already put in your network of contacts.** If you are planning to get involved full-time in Christian ministry, the chances are that you've already had experience in building relationships, whether it is through your family, schooling, work or church life. You already know how to chat to your friends, to invite people to join you in activities. You've probably gone on holidays with friends, argued your side of a discussion, run activities with others. You just need to put these skills that you already have to use as you sit down with a friend and ask them to join you in the adventure that God is calling you into.

Donors, investors or partners?

How you view your supporters and your perspective on their role in your ministry will have a significant bearing on how they view you and the role that they perceive themselves to play in your work. Wherever you set the ceiling will, for most supporters, be the limit of how far they choose to get involved. If you assume that they have a limited role to play, perhaps just giving money and praying for you now and again, then that is the highest they will feel able to aspire to. However, if you offer a higher level of involvement, some among your support team will willingly and enthusiastically rise to the challenge.

Donor

A donor stands apart from the cause, with little effort made to build any meaningful relationship between the giver and the receiver. At its most basic level, it is the relationship between the person shaking the collecting tin on Main Street on a Saturday morning and the passer-by who puts 50p in the tin. The giver may not even be aware which cause they are donating to; the receiver has no interest in the giver, apart from a basic appreciation that at least they gave some money when most others just walked past.

There will be some among your support team who may never get beyond the donor level of involvement. For some reason they choose to give to you, perhaps even monthly, but they have no growing interest in you or your work. But while it is almost a given that you will have some supporters who will settle for this donor-type perspective of you, **what should not be a given is that you settle for a donor-type perspective of them**. If they do choose this basic level of involvement, it should be through their choice, not because you don't offer them options for greater involvement.

Investor

An investor has a greater interest in the cause they support, but the relationship is still distant. If you own a few shares in a publicly listed company, for example, you actually own part of the company. But you might not feel as though you do. Typically, the company sends you updates now and again to tell you how well they are doing, even putting a positive spin on negative news. They plan their AGM, at which you have a vote, at a time and place that is totally inconvenient for you to attend, and the proxy voting forms they send you, as well as the wording of the motions being voted on, are so difficult to understand that you just bin them. But you **own** the company, or at least a bit of it.

The company doesn't really want you interfering in its affairs, but they don't want you to withdraw your investment either, so they adopt a balancing act of keeping you sweet, but at arm's length.

Many missionaries and Christian workers adopt the investor approach to their supporters. They keep them sweet with a few impersonal *'Dear Friends'* prayer letters each year, hope that the supporters will keep giving the money, but also hope that they don't take up too much of their time.

Again, some supporters will settle for this level of involvement, but it should not be because you don't offer them a higher option.

Partner

A partner feels an ownership of whatever it is that they are part of. Whether it is the intensity of a marriage partnership, the obligations of a business partnership or simply the interdependence of being a partner in a sports team, a partner understands that he or she has a special and unique role to play and that without this the marriage, business or team would not function as well as it does.

While each partner may have a very different role to play, some with a higher profile than others, each part is vital to the overall effectiveness of the partnership. A partner knows that if their bit is missing, no matter what their role might be, then the whole entity suffers.

Without the money, prayers and encouragement of your supporters, your ministry simply wouldn't exist. As in our human families, where different members play different parts, each vital to the overall functioning of the family unit, so in God's family each needs to play their role to ensure that the family works to its maximum potential. Not all of your supporters will fully appreciate the partnership role they play in your work. But they should be given the chance, offered opportunities to do something different, encouraged to help in ways they haven't helped before. Then watch to see who responds and build on their growing interest.

Towards the end of the book we will look at some practical ways of working towards this.

Building a support team takes time

One couple who contacted me asking for help had set up their own Christian organisation, confident that God had called them to the work they were doing. Working on the basis that the big gifts would come somehow, someday and from somewhere, they kept spending money they didn't have in pursuit of God's call. By the time I met with them they were £50,000 in debit, mostly held on credit cards, and paying £2,000 per month just in interest! Was it a case of them not hearing God's call correctly? Possibly. But it is just as possible that they had an unrealistic idea about support-raising, assuming that it would magically appear while they got on with the 'real' work.

Building a base of solid, committed supporters is as much part of your 'real' work as any other aspect of your ministry. It isn't an added extra that will somehow work itself out on its own.

To make all this happen takes time, and that's something people often claim not to have. But we all have 24 hours a day. It depends whether we count building and maintaining our support base to be sufficient a priority to warrant our time being spent on it. There are no short-cuts to building relationships. *'Dear Friends'* letters, while they are useful for at least letting people know that you are still around, don't build relationships. ☞ **We need to get some creative ways of helping our supporters move from interest in our work to involvement and from knowing about what we do to understanding what we do and why we do it.**

☞ As a rule of thumb, you should allocate ten per cent of your **working** time on an ongoing basis to relating to your supporter team. Too much? Not if we really consider the supporters to be partners, members of God's family at work with us, not just funders. And a well-spent ten per cent will secure a firm support base for as long as you are involved in Christian ministry.

Moving from managing a branch of Nat West in Greater London to joining the staff of Youth for Christ was a big step for Paul, especially when it meant a serious drop in pay and raising support to cover at least 50 per cent of his new salary. Paul was stepping into a new role of Executive Director of Youth for Christ (YFC), overseeing all the administration and general running of the organisation. He and his wife Val weren't going to some remote, unreached tribal people group. They weren't even going to be working directly with British teenagers. They were going to be in an office, in the Midlands, working on what could be seen as mundane tasks.

Their only experience in raising support had been from the other side of the fence – as supporters themselves. Because they enjoyed being supporters themselves, and had some idea of what they appreciated about the relationships they had with those they supported, Paul and Val simply reversed the roles. Even with some enthusiasm for support-raising, Paul knew that his job was so vast that unless they deliberately carved out time to work on their support, it would always get done "next week, when things are less hectic"! They would have to work both smart and hard to achieve the 50 per cent minimum asked by YFC.

Initially, evenings and weekends were spent with key friends, explaining what God had called them to and asking if they'd like to be part of their support team. They wrote to others who they couldn't get to see personally, often following up their letter with phone calls. When they raised enough support to cover 50 per cent of their salary, Paul and Val simply kept going, and eventually exceeded the 100 per cent figure.

> *And it didn't stop there. Paul and Val understood that their supporters were as much part of their team as those who worked beside them in the YFC office. Developing partnerships with their supporters would need more than just sending the odd prayer letter every few months.*
>
> *They began a routine that ensured that they kept in regular contact with those who had committed to support them. They wrote brief notes to supporters in the early mornings before breakfast; weekends sometimes saw them hosting supporters from the London area; they made sure they phoned a couple of supporters each week in the evenings.*
>
> *While some of these tasks undoubtedly took time, Paul and Val didn't see them as onerous tasks that impinged on their free time, things that had to be done to allow them to get the support they needed to do their job with YFC. Not at all. They saw them as a great way of keeping their friends involved in their lives and ministry – an integral and enjoyable part of their daily work with YFC.*
>
> *Paul and Val subsequently moved on to another leadership role in Christian ministry. In this case there was no expectation on them to raise support, with the salary being paid from the central funds of the organisation. But the relationships that they had built up with their supporters during their years with Youth for Christ were too important to simply end in mid-stream, so they asked their supporters if they would like to switch their support to the new organisation, designating it towards their salary. A good number of their supporters did so. Paul and Val were pleased to keep the relationships going; the supporters were happy that their input was still wanted; the new organisation was happy getting a new staff member who brought some of his salary with him, even though it wasn't a requirement.*

How you view a task often determines how you feel about it and, ultimately, your decision about whether or not you will do it today or postpone it to a later (and frequently never reached) date.

SUMMARY

- Building a base of committed supporters is as much part of your work as any other aspect of your ministry.

- God has made sure your supporters are already there and that there is enough money for you to do what he is asking of you.

- But don't assume that they will simply appear without you going out to look for them!

- Support-raising is not a science; it's an art of building relationships.

- You already have the skills you need to build a support team.

- Your view of your supporters will greatly determine how they view both you and their role in your work.

- Building up and sustaining a support team takes time and you should allocate ten per cent of your working time to it.

CHAPTER 4

HOW DO SUPPORTERS DECIDE TO SUPPORT YOU?

We all have a process that we use in making decisions. Sometimes we're conscious of it, sometimes we're not. Depending on the importance or urgency of the decision, sometimes the whole process takes just a few seconds; at other times it can take days, weeks or months.

Hopefully people won't take weeks or months when deciding whether or not they will support you, but they will go through some mental process nonetheless.

The decision-making ladder

This diagram shows the basic stages a person can be at in their decision about your support. It's not an exact science, but it gives some idea of the process people go through in order to make an informed decision about supporting you.

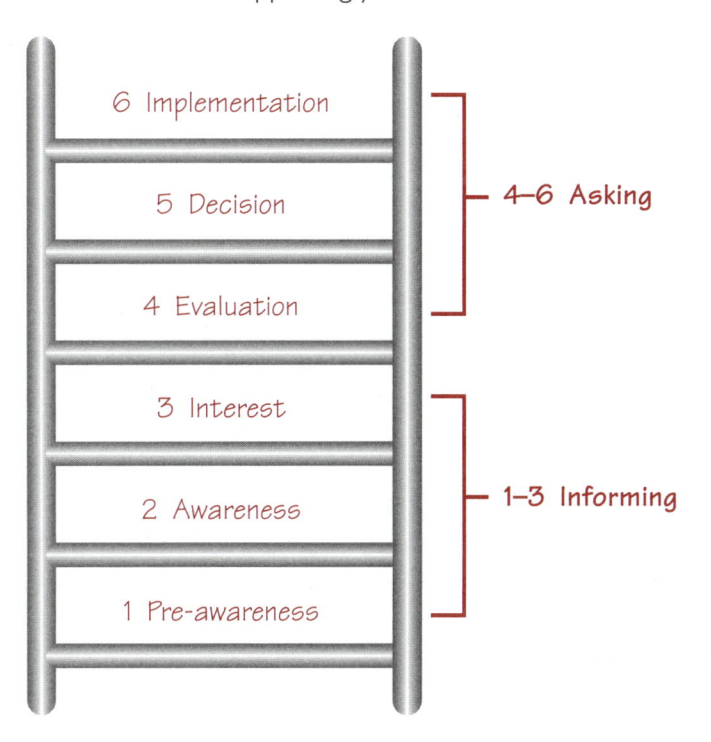

```
6 Implementation
5 Decision          ⎫
4 Evaluation        ⎬ 4–6 Asking
3 Interest          ⎫
2 Awareness         ⎬ 1–3 Informing
1 Pre-awareness     ⎭
```

Let's take a look at each stage on the decision-making ladder.

1 Pre-awareness

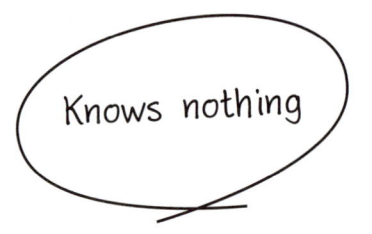

(Knows nothing)

This is someone who has no awareness at all that you are getting involved full-time in Christian ministry. It may be somebody you haven't seen since you left school or college, or perhaps someone you used to work with or attend church with who has moved elsewhere. You might have been close at one time, and you could probably track each other down if you wanted, but there hasn't been any real contact for some time.

I know it seems too obvious to mention, **but it could also be someone you haven't met yet**. Obviously they would have no idea at all about you or your decision to raise support to follow God's call on your life. But you'll be surprised at the number of your supporters who seem to appear from nowhere and start supporting you. **Remember, it is more about their need to give than it is your need to receive.** God may well have his hand on some people who, for whatever reason, need to give more and he may choose to bring them across your path so that their need can be fulfilled. There are no distant cousins in God's family, only brothers and sisters you don't know yet.

2 Awareness

(Knows a little bit)

This person has some idea that you are planning to do some sort of Christian work, but don't push them on the details. This could be someone in your church who you don't know very well. They vaguely remember that you're heading off to do something with young people. Maybe you're going to work with Child Evangelism Fellowship somewhere in Europe? Or maybe it was Youth for Christ in Birmingham? Or maybe they're mixing you up with somebody else who was talked about in church last month? Whatever their understanding (or lack of it), they certainly have no concept that your plans merit any specific response from them.

3 Interest

Knows a bit more and shows some interest

Someone at this next step up the ladder has either expressed some interest in your plans or your relationship with them is strong enough for you to assume an interest. It could be someone in your house group at church, a Christian colleague at work, or a friend who has watched your progress into Christian ministry with interest. They are genuinely pleased for you, probably ask some intelligent questions, maybe even express some concern at the risks they perceive you to be taking. But for all their interest, it hasn't actually struck them that they could have a key role to play as part of your support team. They mightn't even be all that clear about how your work will be funded, perhaps assuming that you'll 'just get paid' by whatever organisation you work with.

4 Evaluation

Knows enough to make a decision

By the time someone reaches this point, they don't need any more information, but they may need help to organise the information they have into a clear picture. They know that you are going into Christian ministry and could probably give a good basic explanation of what it is that you are planning to do. They also are aware that you need financial support from your friends to make it happen. They might even have given the possibility of supporting you some fleeting thought, but the busyness of life means that they haven't got round to doing anything about it.

It's as if they have all the pieces of a jigsaw puzzle, but haven't had the time (or motivation) to put them all together to make up the full picture. If they did, they'd find their face in the middle of it, alongside yours, as part of the overall package that is required to ensure that you follow God's call on your life.

5 Decision

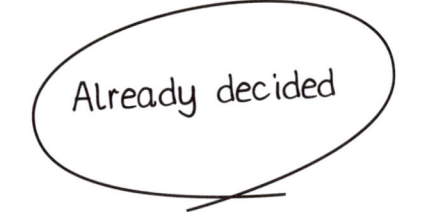

(Already decided)

This person has actually decided to support you and may have even told you. But they haven't done anything about it.

It might have been right at the beginning, when you first started exploring the option of Christian ministry that they said, *"When it all gets worked out, we'll support you"*. Or maybe they sidled up to you in church one Sunday after you'd spoken about your plans and said that they'd like to support you, but then they walked off leaving their decision just hanging there, and you aren't sure what to do about it.

Another possibility is that they have decided to support you but they haven't told you and haven't actually got round to giving anything yet. The problem is, you've no way of knowing.

6 Implementation

(Started giving)

This person has not only decided to support you, they have filled in a standing order form or sent in their first cheque. You have some realistic understanding of their commitment, whether it is to be part of your support team on an ongoing basis or perhaps simply giving a special gift at the outset to get you started. This understanding isn't just guesswork on your part.

Inviting people up the ladder

Naturally, you'd like to see as many people as possible at the top of the ladder and there are some things you can do to encourage people to take the next steps on the way up. What you can't change is where people are starting from. During your support-raising, you will probably be concentrating on those at the high end of the 'interest' stage and at the 'evaluation' stage, while looking for ways of encouraging those at the lower stages to take steps up. You will also need to ensure that those at the 'decision' stage get the chance to actually give what they've decided to give and that those who are already on board are well appreciated and kept up-to-date with your progress.

The higher up the ladder you go, the more personal the process becomes. It is relatively easy to inform people with brochures, by speaking at meetings and the like. **But when you really want a specific individual to give serious consideration to becoming part of your support team, nothing beats sitting down and asking them directly.** It's like at church when someone makes an announcement to the effect that people need to sign up by the following week for some forthcoming event. By the time the service is over, too many of those who had intended to sign the sheet have either forgotten or got sidetracked.

However, if whoever made the announcement stands at the back of the church at the end of the service, individually encouraging people to go to the event and guiding them to the sign-up sheet, then there will be a much higher response rate. This is balancing the information in the announcement with specific and personalised asking to ensure the maximum success. It might feel a bit more embarrassing for the person organising the event to be so specific with people, but in the end many more people will attend.

Up close and personal

Too often we hide behind a general and more impersonal approach with the (often vain) hope that the right people will understand what we need, overcome all the obstacles that make it difficult for them to connect with us and offer their wholehearted support. Yes, the more personal the process becomes, the more uncomfortable it is for the asker. **But the more positive the outcome is.** And, what's more, the more personal the approach, the more the potential supporter understands that it is them in particular that you want to support you, not just anyone who might respond to a comment at a meeting or a brochure they pick up from an information table.

☞ **So by all means, ensure that people are well informed about your plans and your work. But don't just leave it there.** By building on the information with specific approaches to those with the highest interest, you will be helping them fulfil what they really want to do, but may well never get round to doing unless you take the initiative.

Sometimes people will appear out of the blue and run right up to the top of the ladder with amazing speed. You need to keep your eye open for these opportunities, because they are often more to do with the giver needing to give than they are to do with your need for support.

> *Elaine worked at Operation Mobilisation's main British training base in Halesowen in the West Midlands. She'd been a bit rushed this particular morning, so she was doing her normal morning Bible reading on the bus on her way to work. The girl who sat beside her on the bus asked, "Excuse me, are you a Christian?" "Yes," Elaine replied, "are you?" She was. It transpired that the girl (Sandra) worked in a bank and had recently been transferred to the Halesowen branch. She didn't really like the area that much, hadn't felt settled and hadn't yet found a church she enjoyed. She was beginning to think that moving here had been a mistake. Sandra poured all this out to Elaine, delighted to find someone who listened with genuine interest.*
>
> *Sandra then asked what Elaine did. "I work with Operation Mobilisation here in Halesowen. Have you ever heard of them?" "Yes," Sandra replied, "you're the people with the ships, aren't you?" Elaine explained that, yes they were the people with the ships (seems everybody knew about OM's ships!) but that OM's main UK training base was in Halesowen.*
>
> *Sandra was quite excited to find out that God hadn't abandoned Halesowen after all. In the course of a brief conversation about OM and the training work that Elaine did, Sandra asked, "How are OM staff funded?" It would have been so easy for Elaine to say something like, "Oh, the Lord provides for us" or perhaps, "I receive support from my home church, some family members and some friends". Both of these would have been true.*
>
> *But Elaine was beginning to see that there was more to this 'chance' meeting than met the eye. So she replied, "I'm supported by people just like you – Christians interested in seeing God's Kingdom extended." She then added, "You could support me if you'd like." She went on to explain briefly what it would involve. Sandra was more than happy to explore the possibility, so they arranged to meet for lunch later in the week. She signed up to support Elaine on a monthly basis.*

There are 101 logical reasons why this wasn't a good support appointment. Elaine and Sandra had never met each other before, they knew nothing about each other, Sandra knew very little about OM, it was early in the morning – on a bus, on the way to work!

But Elaine saw beyond normal logic. She saw there were the fingerprints of God all over the encounter.

It wasn't about Elaine and her need for support. It was about Sandra and her need to feel that there was a reason that God had placed her in Halesowen. Because Elaine took the risk that God might be doing something unusual, it allowed Sandra to rocket up the decision-making ladder at breakneck speed. If Elaine hadn't taken the risk and had deflected the early-morning conversation away from the supposedly embarrassing topic of financial support, then there would be no story to tell. Except that God would have looked elsewhere for someone to help meet Sandra's needs.

Try rewriting this story from Sandra's perspective

I was on my way to work one morning, feeling a bit down, when I sat beside a girl reading her Bible on the bus...

A note about corporate givers

Corporate givers make decisions differently from individual givers. By individual givers I mean people who make decisions about their own money – basically, your friends and other individuals you will approach for support. Corporate givers make decisions on behalf of others who provide the money – church committees, trustees and other groups. Individual givers can make decisions quickly.

For example, if you were to ask me for support today, I'd need to check with Phyllis, take a quick look at our budget and give it a bit of thought and prayer. But there's no reason why I couldn't decide within a day or two. Corporate givers, on the other hand, often need time to meet, discuss, consider other requests, to ensure that your request falls in line with the interests and/or guidelines of those whose money they are entrusted to disburse. It could take several months before they get all the ducks in a row and give you a definitive answer. And you may well be asked more questions before you get an answer. Or you may not get a definitive answer at all and be left scratching your head wondering what to do next.

☞ **Involve the group from as early on in the process as you can**, especially your home church and other churches where you have been a member. Ask about the decision-making process and play by their rules. And make sure that your voice is heard when the decision-making group meets by spending time with those on the group who are most positively disposed towards you and your cause. Remember, the group will be discussing other funding requests at the same meeting, so you need to be well represented to ensure that your case is adequately heard.

CHAPTER 5

WHY DO SUPPORTERS DECIDE TO SUPPORT YOU?

People will support you for a mixture of reasons. Your need for support will act as the trigger for their giving, but meeting your financial need is unlikely to be their main motivating factor. There will be a mixture of motivations milling around in their minds as they choose. The following story shows that sometimes the motivations may be complex, entirely personal and impossible for anyone other than God to predict.

> Some years ago, Campus Crusade's leadership in Lebanon responded to a sudden deterioration in the country's stability by recommending that family members who could leave the country should do so. The wife and children of one leader's family hastily moved to Egypt, while he remained in Beirut. There was no budget for this unexpected move, so Campus Crusade in Ireland undertook to fund this family's relocation.
>
> Since we had no spare cash ourselves as an organisation, a number of us contacted our supporters asking them for help. I was very surprised to get a cheque for £3,000 from a supporter whose support for us was £300 per year. He was a well-respected Christian businessman I had only met a couple of times and who had been introduced to me by another supporter.
>
> Intrigued by his decision to give ten times more to this need than he was giving to us, I asked him why. His answer surprised me more than his gift did. He told me that he and his wife were planning to separate. Almost no one knew this, apart from very close family and the leader of his church – and now me! He said that he felt so sad for the couple in Lebanon who were being forced by circumstances to live apart, while he and his wife were making the choice to split simply because their marriage had run out of steam. He asked me to let him know of any other family-related need that I came across, promising to do what he could to help.

> *If you had asked me prior to this what I thought he might be interested in giving an extra gift to, although I didn't know him that well, I wouldn't have guessed that it would be family-type needs. But God knew that he needed some way of responding to the disappointment and discouragement he felt about his own difficult family situation and gave me just enough of a relationship with him to innocently ask for his help.*
>
> *Over the following years he gave to a number of other family-type needs that I put to him. Even better, he and his wife worked through their difficulties and didn't split up. Although I still don't really know him well, I'm one of only a few people who have any idea that marriage break-up was an option – all because I stumbled across something God was doing in his life by asking him to help a family that neither of us had even met. It's clearly about a lot more than money.*

On the following pages you'll find some of the possible reasons why someone might choose to support you – some good, some not so good.

Historic relationship – *continuing an existing investment*

This is the number one reason people will support you, especially at the outset. These are your friends, the people in whom you've invested time and energy, the people who know you and like you, the people you send birthday cards to. It isn't that it is logical that they'd want to support you. It would be illogical for them not to. If the position were reversed, and they were joining a Christian organisation where they were raising support, of course you would want to support them. Some of these potential supporters may be so keen to be on your support team that they approach you first. But others don't quite get round to it.

It is so easy to put off contacting those we are closest to – the fear of rejection by our friends can paralyse us into inactivity.

Susie was raising support to work with Latin Link, a mission agency with a special focus on Latin America. Her support target seemed daunting, but as she began contacting people she thought might be interested in her future work, she was pleasantly surprised by their response and she was making steady progress towards her target.

The one person she couldn't bring herself to ask was Linda, her best friend and flat-mate. She felt that if she asked her, Linda would feel obliged to say yes. The relationship meant too much to Susie to put it under that amount of threat. She hoped that Linda would take the initiative and offer to support her.

One morning, over their usual rushed breakfast, Linda asked Susie what was wrong with their relationship. Stunned by what seemed like a bolt right out of the blue, Susie stammered some reply about everything being OK, there was no problem.

But there was a problem, insisted Linda. "You've been asking all sorts of people about supporting you, but you haven't asked me – what's the problem?"

Sometimes we can damage a relationship by being overprotective of it, especially when we allow our emotions to convince ourselves that someone close to us would feel pressured into supporting us, when we know that we'd be more than happy to support them if the position were reversed. In this case, it all got resolved, Linda got to be part of Susie's support team and Susie learned a valuable lesson.

Partners – *part of something worthwhile*

Many of your supporters have lives that are hectic but may nevertheless feel flat. Their church activities are caught up with their domestic chores and they may be left wondering if they are contributing anything really worthwhile to God's Kingdom.

By connecting with you, no matter what you are doing, your supporters are given a sense of being part of something worthwhile. You might not think of your work as being in any way exciting, but from where the supporter sits, it looks it. Given that we are all called by God (or at least should be) to be partners in his family's business, whether it is as a supporter or as a Christian worker, the perception that your work has more significance than theirs is not true. But it is still their perception and therefore true for them. As you build your relationship with the supporter over the years, you will have opportunities to correct the misperceptions about missionaries being at the top of the spiritual food-chain, but what you can't do is change how they think about the process at the outset.

> *I was running a support training day for some of Interserve's UK-based staff. Unlike Interserve missionaries working throughout Asia and the Middle East, these weren't people who saw themselves as being at the 'coalface' of mission work. They were mostly office-based staff who spent their days on the phone, sitting at computers or in meetings.*
>
> *I was having difficulty convincing them that their jobs would be viewed as significant by their supporters. Right at this point one of the staff arrived, about two hours after we had started. She apologised for arriving late, explaining that she had got delayed at the embassy of a country normally resistant to traditional mission work where she'd been negotiating a visa for one of their staff. It was normal, everyday, run-of-the-mill work for her and for her colleagues, but how many of her friends could even have pointed out that particular country on a world map?*
>
> *Don't underestimate the significance your work brings to the lives of your supporters.*

Vicarious – involvement through others

Some people will support you because they can't do what you do, but can still be actively involved in Christian mission by being part of your support team. It might be an older person who simply doesn't have the energy to be as involved as they once were, or someone whose personal circumstances mean they cannot be as active as they would like to be. Their support for you is as much about fulfilling their need to continue to feel part of what God is doing as it is about helping you.

> In February 2001 my mother celebrated her 80th birthday. She was still quite fit and healthy, but the reality of the facts on her birth certificate were beginning to tell. Her energy levels weren't what they used to be and she felt left behind by the quickening pace of change in society. In particular, she felt unable to communicate effectively with teenagers and young people. Our home used to be full of teens and twenties when we were growing up, so this inability to identify with those 60-70 years younger than her was a frustration. She loved young people, knew that Jesus loved them, but she didn't like today's youth culture, hadn't understood its music since the mid-60s and felt that she could no longer talk a language they would understand.
>
> We convinced her to have a big party to celebrate her 80th birthday, inviting as many of her current and past friends as we could. Although initially a bit reluctant, she warmed to the idea when she found out that her only daughter was coming back from Namibia for the occasion. Given that her shelves at home were already laden down with ornaments, and at 80 she already had all she needed and wanted, she asked that those coming to the party bring a cash gift instead of a present. Not for her, I hasten to add. The gifts were all given to her church and were disbursed at her request to four different **Christian youth organisations**, not Help the Aged, Age Concern or any other group that helped people like her.
>
> This was my mother's way of still sharing the gospel with teenagers, years after she felt unable to do so in any direct way.

Giving to those active in Christian ministry brings great satisfaction to the lives of those who, for whatever reason, genuinely cannot get as involved as they would like to be, especially the elderly.

Want to accomplish a particular purpose – *my money will help*

Sometimes people will support you because they share your commitment to the particular cause you are working for. It could be that you are planning to work with young people and the potential supporter shares that passion through their involvement in a local drop-in centre run by their church. Or maybe it is a school teacher who can empathise with your decision to work in a mission school in Asia. Whatever the connection, what you are doing strikes a chord with a keen interest of the supporter.

We all wish that all our supporters could be as committed to our cause as we are. But most supporters are primarily committed to us, at least initially. Their commitment to, and involvement in, our cause may grow with time. A few, however, will start out already interested in the cause itself. Their support for you means that they can achieve much more in a cause that is important to them than they could do on their own.

Guilt – *responding to social or spiritual concerns*

This is one of the negative motivations that is sometimes in the mind of a supporter. It most often surfaces if you are involved in some emotive aspect of ministry, perhaps working with some of the world's poorest and marginalised people. The amount of wealth we have in the west, both in comparative and real terms, is massive.

Sometimes, when people with plenty are personally confronted with a situation where their help is needed to alleviate the needs of those with very little, the only way they can deal with the guilt of their own wealth is to give. It gets you the money, but not always the real heart commitment.

However, some people may respond with genuine compassion to a cause that is emotive. For example, if you work with children whose lives are lived in abject poverty in a land where they receive no help and where they have no hope, then a couple in the affluent west, whose own children want for nothing, may well feel compassion for those children you are reaching out to help. In this sort of scenario, you should not shy away from being open about the emotive aspects of your cause. But be careful not to use the potential supporters' compassion to make them feel guilty if they choose not to support you. Your cause, no matter how heart-tugging it may be, does not automatically mean that God wants the potential supporter to give to you.

Self-worth – *need to achieve or maintain self-image*

Another of the negative motivations. We see it in churches, libraries and other public buildings that are named after the person or family who provided the money: a permanent and very public reminder to all who pass by of the generosity of the giver.

You're not likely to be the beneficiary of the sort of gift that would build a library, but you might still meet this motivation in other forms. It is the person who not only gives, but keeps reminding you about it. Maybe they bought you that much-needed laptop, and then for years afterwards ask how it's doing. They might even introduce you to others as their missionary friends for whom they bought a laptop when you first started out. Or maybe it's the person who supports you simply because they found out that someone else with whom they are in a social climbing race is supporting you. Remember, though, that none of us have totally pure motives about all the decisions we make.

Because they love Christ – *Christian gratitude*

Supporters like these are both a delight and a frustration. They are a delight because they are so full of thankfulness to God for who he is and what he has done, that they overflow with enthusiasm for the work of God's Kingdom.

They are a frustration because they often really don't care too much about what you're involved in. They would never admit to it, but it's the case nevertheless. They just love God so much that they want to give to him. Because they can't give directly to God, you're the best they can find!

> We had an old Godly lady who supported us for years. She was a family friend who had watched me grow up and had prayed for me throughout my entire life. We tried to get to see her at least once a year and she would always welcome us with great delight, eager to hear what we were doing. Then she would launch into a story about a neighbour she'd had the chance to witness to, or a passage of scripture that meant a lot to her, or a book that she'd read recently, or an inspiring speaker she'd heard. Every half hour or so she would say, "Well, what have you been up to?" and then launch into something else that God was teaching her.
>
> After a couple of hours we would leave, well informed about all that God was doing in and through her life, but with little or no chance to explain what we were doing. I used to get frustrated with this. I wanted her to know that her support was helping push back the frontiers of God's kingdom, or whatever else I was up to at the time. But it really didn't matter to her. She knew us and trusted us. Her support was an expression of her love for God. In truth, it had very little to do with us.

Meet specific needs – *like to see the results*

Every now and again a supporter will say to you, *"If you ever have any special needs, let us know."* So, how do you handle this? What exactly do they mean – a toothbrush or a Rolls Royce?

Most people segment their giving into regular and special. Even if they don't do it consciously, they do it sub-consciously. There are also supporters who like to be able to respond to urgent or special needs: 'fixer-types'. They hear about a need on a Monday, send you a cheque on the Tuesday, you get it on the Wednesday, you sort the problem on the Thursday, tell them it's sorted on the Friday, they're happy at the weekend!

Supporters like this may not be particularly wealthy, but they can often be people who understand the vagaries of cash flow and unexpected expenses.

Assuming their comment wasn't just a throwaway remark, you should take them at their word. Yes, you will feel nervous, maybe even embarrassed, calling them up to explain about your unexpected need. **But imagine how they will feel** if they hear long afterwards that you cancelled going to that training conference, didn't buy the laptop you needed, turned down the chance to go on a special project, all because you didn't have the money you needed, and you didn't let them help.

We are talking about unbudgeted and unexpected opportunities or emergencies that, if you can fund them, will benefit your work. You didn't know about them in advance and they certainly didn't know either. Do them a favour; give them a call. You can say something like, *"Hello Alex, this is Sam. A couple of months back you said to let you know if I ever had a special need. Well, something has just cropped up this week and I'd like to see if you could help. I've been offered the chance to do a course next month that will be a great help in preparing me for the new responsibilities I'm taking up in the New Year* (or whatever the need is). *The main benefits of me being able to do the course are* (explain how meeting the need you have outlined will help your work). *The total cost of the course, including accommodation, will be £750. At this stage I have about £200 that I can put to it, but I really need to be able to confirm whether or not I can sign up by the end of the week. Because you said to get in touch if I had a need, I didn't want to bypass you on this. Is there any way you could help?"*

In most cases people will be willing to do what they can to help. After all, it was their idea, not yours, that you contact them if you had a need. It is treating the supporter as a partner, not just a donor. Even if their circumstances have changed drastically and they can't help, at least they will appreciate you taking them at their word.

To do

Ring Alex re: course costs

Blessing – *thanksgiving for what God has given them*

Kevin and Lucy were raising support to join an evangelism organisation working in the UK. Living as they did in prosperous suburbia, they were taking quite a drop in income to follow God's call on their lives. They were a little surprised when Jonathan, a new Christian who had just recently started coming to their church agreed to support them. They were even more surprised when Jonathan mentioned the amount he wanted to give. To make sure, Kevin went over the details with him again.

Was the amount he had mentioned an annual amount? "No," came the reply, "it's monthly."

Did he realise that they were looking for supporters who would continue their support over the long-term, not just for a few months? Yes, he was up for ongoing support. Was he sure he could afford it?

At this point Jonathan told them his story.

He was very successful in his business life and had reached the top of the ladder in his chosen career. But his personal life was in pieces. His marriage had broken up, he was depressed, feeling alone and rejected. Living a double life, in public he was the successful businessman, the envy of all his colleagues; in private he was in utter despair.

Living like this eventually got too much for him and he drove down to the coast one evening, planning to end his life. Just as he was about to walk out into the sea and end it all, a dog ran barking across the beach at him. When the owner, a local Christian, realised that his dog was barking at a stranger, he came over to apologise for its behaviour. Finding the man in floods of tears, he realised that something was seriously wrong. That God-ordained encounter led to the man trusting Christ and beginning to get his life sorted out.

"I've lived the first half of my life for myself," Jonathan went on, "and made a mess of it. God has not only spared my physical life, he has given me eternal life too. I want to make sure that I live the rest of the days God gives me according to his agenda and this includes how I use my money. In the past I spent money on myself without ever giving God a thought. I've a lot of catching up to do. I'm so grateful for all that God has done for me. Please take the money."

Whose need was greater? The need of Kevin and Lucy to receive the support or Jonathan's need to give the support?

Although it was an unexpectedly large amount for the limited nature of the relationship, **it was the giver whose needs were most met**.

This story is more dramatic than most and, although the basic elements are true, I've changed almost all the personal details to protect the identity of those involved. But people sometimes do give out of thankfulness for something special that God has done in their lives. They are not trying to pay God back, just expressing thanks in a way that they can. And they might want to express their thanks through you.

Is their support some measure of how important they view your ministry? No, it is a measure of their thankfulness to God. In fact, you are largely irrelevant to the giver. It is God they are expressing their thanks to; you just happened to be there when they wanted to express it. Humbling, isn't it?

Security – *buying favour with God*

We know that our salvation is an undeserved gift from God, but we often have an insane urge to add something to the equation ourselves: something to make God love us more, like us better and think better of us. Daft I know, but we all do it to some extent or other, especially if we feel that we have let God down somehow. It is Satan's classic way of undermining our whole relationship with God.

Some supporters may have this as their motivation. What is more, they might even tell you. Maybe they haven't shared their faith with anybody for years. Maybe they turned down the chance to go into Christian ministry themselves years ago and still feel guilty about it. By supporting you they think that it equalises things, sorts out the balance in their relationship with God.

Again, this is a negative motivation, and you are only likely to become aware of it as the supporter expresses some aspect of their life that they feel isn't up to scratch during a discussion about your support. Where you can, use the opportunity to explore this further with the supporter, helping them recognise their cross-bought worth to God.

Is there a danger in someone using their support for you as a way of trying to make God feel better about them? Yes, there might be that danger. But at least you have the opportunity to help the person get a better grasp of their position in Christ, an opportunity you wouldn't have had if you hadn't been discussing your support with them.

What about people who give with negative motivations?

First of all, we need to recognise that we are not responsible for their motivations. That is between them and God.

Secondly, we need to make sure that we don't feed any negative motivations by how we present our ministry, for example, making people feel guilty if they don't give. Sometimes we can end up doing this without even realising it. In Chapter 8 we'll look at some of the ways this can happen and suggest ways of avoiding it.

Finally, negative giving motivations can be a symptom of some spiritual issues that may need attention. Where appropriate, use the opportunity afforded by the discussion about your support to explore these issues further.

> ☞ **Raising support is a fantastic win-win situation. Everybody gets their needs met. We do great out of it, getting money, prayers and encouragement. They do even better, with their needs met, their account with God credited and more blessings than they can cope with!**

SUMMARY

I grew up in a strict, hell-fire preaching church. One of the visiting preachers in particular used to terrify me as a child. I'm sure he was really a kindly man, with good motives in his preaching, but to me he seemed enormous, with a big black Bible, big black suit and a scowl on his face as he preached. When he wanted to emphasise a point he would stare over his glasses at someone in the congregation and say with great accentuation: *"May the Lord scratch this on your eyeballs!"* meaning, I assume, may you see all the rest of the message through the focus of that main point.

Well, if there is one point to scratch on your eyeballs from this whole book, one point to build your support-raising around, it is this: *Your supporters need to support you more than you need to receive their support.*

- **Remember Jesus' comment that it is more blessed to give than receive?**
- **Remember Paul's note to the Philippians reminding them that their giving to him added to *their* account and ensured that *their* needs got met?**
- **Remember Paul's cajoling of the Corinthians to give to the relief fund for Jerusalem where he stresses the benefit to them without once mentioning the need of those the gift was designed to help?**
- **Remember in Malachi when God told his people that they wouldn't have enough room for all the blessings he would pour out on them if they gave as they were supposed to?**

These promises of God should be enough to convince us. If all you did was allow this reality into your head and heart, then it really will take a lot of the pressure off your support-raising. If all you can do at this stage is get it into your head, that's fine. Pray that God will move it that long journey from head to heart.

Notes

CHAPTER 6

WHY WE DON'T ALWAYS FEEL COMFORTABLE RAISING SUPPORT

So, if the person raising support wins and the person giving the support wins even more, how come the whole process can feel so uncomfortable at times?

There are lots of reasons, any number of which could be in play at the same time:

"If only my ministry sounded more exciting"

One of Satan's specialities is to turn our eyes away from how God has made us right through the cross and to focus them instead on what we see as being wrong with us.

Let's suppose that we know each other slightly. Maybe we go to the same church or know each other through work. I have £50 per month to give and I'm seeing you this evening to hear about your work. Tomorrow I'm meeting Mark and Lorna, who I know equally well, to hear about their work with children who are born, live and die in the sewers of a major city in India. I've decided that I want to be as committed as I can to one or the other, so I'm not going to split the amount. **Explain to me why you should get it.**

Take a few moments now to think through what you would say.

How did you do?

If you simply said that I should give it to Mark and Lorna, then maybe you are confusing emotion with God's call. Whatever God has called you to do is his call for you. It is as valid as any other aspect of the work of his Kingdom, even if it isn't as emotive. By simply assuming that the most emotive cause is automatically the one that I should give to denies me, as the giver, the chance to explore what God might be calling me to get involved in. As a potential giver, I need to hear your heart, understand your need and then make my own decision before God.

We can get caught in the *'if only'* syndrome. If only my ministry were more exciting. If only my church were more mission-minded. If only my church weren't already supporting so many missionaries. If only my family were more wealthy. If only I were more outgoing. If only I had more friends in good jobs. Every time you say *'if only'* you are saying that God has made a mistake: placed you in the wrong family, or in the wrong ministry, or in the wrong church, or with the wrong friends, or with the wrong personality. He hasn't. He is more aware of who you are than even you are. Yet he has chosen you to do something specific for his Kingdom. Don't let Satan rob you of the security and confidence of being in the centre of God's will.

☞ **When you speak to potential supporters, don't downplay the importance of your work. I don't mean that you should overwhelm people with a sense of crisis, but if someone is going to give you money every month to do whatever it is that God has called you to, there needs to be some sense of it being significant, of your work meeting the needs of people, whether directly or indirectly. Try to communicate the passion that God has put in your heart for what it is he has called you to. If you are too 'ho-hum' in the way you explain your ministry to people, they may think that you simply want an easy job, around nice people who don't smoke or swear (well, not too much) and who do some good in the world.**

Luke 15 says that the angels have a party in heaven when someone repents, presumably with great singing and dancing. In some way, what you are doing is helping generate the heavenly equivalent of Riverdance. If you don't have a real, God-given passion for what you are doing and the people your work will ultimately benefit, or if you've lost that passion over the years, ask God to give it to you.

"What if they say no... or yes!?"

What will happen if we ask someone we know for support and they say no? Will this damage our relationship? What happens if they say yes? Will this create a dependent relationship?

Generally, but not always, women are better at developing and maintaining peer relationships than men. Just take a look at how much easier it is to arrange a women's meeting in church than a men's meeting. Men need a special reason – the Monthly Saturday Morning Breakfast After Football Prayer Meeting. Women can meet without having to invent a reason.

We carry this into support-raising. Some people are so over-cautious of relationships that they don't make any direct contact with anyone, hoping that the fact that the information is available will, in itself, be enough to get people to sign up. The organised or persistent few might, but in today's busy world, with so much competition for any spare moments of time and energy, many who might actually be interested in supporting you simply won't get round to it, especially if it involves them chasing the process themselves.

Then there are the others at the other end of the spectrum, with no concept of relationship, who just work through the church directory, asking everyone A–Z without giving much thought to why they are asking that particular person.

Most of us are somewhere between these two extremes, probably veering towards the over-cautious end of the scale. ☞ **Wherever you are, work towards the middle.** If you are over-hasty, prepared to contact anyone and everyone for support, slow down and ask yourself, *Why am I asking this particular person for support? What do I already know about them that would lead me to believe that they would be interested? What is there in their life that makes a connection with me and the work I'll be doing?* If you still think that it might be a good match, then fine, go ahead. But if you can't really think of any reason why they might be interested in supporting you, then maybe it's time to back off.

If you are towards the over-cautious end of the scale, take some chances. Think about those you are not contacting directly because you're too nervous about what it might do to the relationship. Do you think that they might be interested in supporting you? If they were the people raising support, would you want to support them? Given the busyness of people's lives, are you making it too difficult for people to

Why we don't always feel comfortable raising support

sign up? ☞ Try approaching some of those who know and trust you enough to still accept you, even if you blow it with them. Ask them not only to consider supporting you, but if they minded you approaching them. If your friends are like you, they are most likely to say that, no, they didn't mind being approached, but that they couldn't do it themselves!

Ask anyone who has lived on a support basis for some years. They will tell you that, yes, there were some people who they expected to support them who didn't and the relationship has cooled off a bit. But they will also tell you of others who began supporting them when they hardly knew them and who they would now count as good friends. In spite of our attempts to freeze relationships in time, they are always on the move. Remember that good friend at school, the one you thought would be a friend for life? The one you've no idea where they are today?

> ☞ **For some, choosing whether or not to support you will be a defining moment in your relationship. A few may slip more into the background because they see their commitments elsewhere. Many others will grow and develop beyond your wildest dreams because they choose to be committed to you.**

"It can't be done"

Saying *"It can't be done"* isn't doubt and it isn't uncertainty. It is unbelief. It is saying that your support target is too big for God. For many, facing their initial support target can be a daunting task. In reality, the total amounts they are raising are likely to be less than the gross family income in their previous jobs. But it still seems huge. Be careful not to settle for *"It can't be done"*.

> *I was working with a couple who had been with a major international mission for 20 years. They had never had 100 per cent support, and had rarely got above 80 per cent. Even with 100 per cent, they certainly wouldn't have been rich, but they*

would have had enough to live and work effectively. For years the mission agency didn't pay much attention to the couple's financial situation and the couple themselves assumed that they would never have enough support to do all that God was calling them to. Yes, they had enough for the essentials, but other aspects of their life and work remained unexplored. Holidays were out of the question. The car was as often off the road as it was running. Projects that they'd have loved to get involved in passed them by. It wasn't that they wanted to live like this; they just thought that there was no other option for them.

Eventually the mission began to take their situation seriously, setting deadlines for the couple to get to 100 per cent. Seeing this as the chance to escape their unbelief, they took risks, began approaching people they should have contacted years before. God responded, bringing in new support from unexpected sources also. Within a matter of months the couple reached 100 per cent support, for the first time ever. Their delight was tempered with regret. Regret that they had spent 20 years in unbelief, not trusting that God could do it.

If God calls you, he will provide for you. This doesn't mean that your support will fall into your lap from some sort of heavenly parachute. For every time of excitement and encouragement as you raise your support, there may well be times of disappointment and despondency. But never lose sight of God, his word and his promises. He will always fulfil his promises, although perhaps not always according to our plan and our timetable.

On a flight out of Belfast one morning, I was sitting in an aisle seat, with a mother and young daughter in the middle and window seats. It was the child's first flight and she was really excited. As we took off and soared above the Belfast hills, she exclaimed, *"Mummy, those mountains aren't as big from up here!"* To a small child, Cavehill and Black Mountain can seem enormous when you're staring up at them from the bottom. But getting above them gave her a completely different perspective.

So it can be with your support. When you're at the bottom looking up at your target, it can seem enormous, sometimes so big that it can eclipse your view of God. But when you look at it from above, from God's perspective, *"Those mountains aren't as big from up here!"*

"I feel too uncomfortable doing this"

Comfort zones are oddly shaped. Each of us has bits of our comfort zones that bulge with experience and practice; things we can do in our sleep. Other bits, by comparison, are positively skeletal; tasks and skills we have never done before, where we feel beyond our comfort zone very quickly. Sometimes it doesn't really matter how well we develop the particular new skill. Becoming totally proficient in a new hobby, while very satisfying, isn't really a life or death issue. In other situations, like mastering a new skill required in our job, the implications are more significant. And it seems that the more important it is to master the new skill, the more uncomfortable you feel in the process.

Raising support is likely to leave you feeling outside your comfort zone. It is a task in which you may well not be experienced and in which you might not have had a lot of training. And it is vital to the future of what God has called you to.

At this point you have two options.

Because raising support makes you feel uncomfortable, you can simply give up and retreat inside your existing comfort areas. This is one reason why some people apply to work with organisations where they do not get to raise support. But if that's the main factor in determining God's call on your life, it's a dangerous direction to look for guidance.

The other option when faced with a task that is both inevitable and uncomfortable is to broaden your comfort zone until it encompasses whatever it is that you need to do. If you're working your way through this book, the likelihood is that you really have no other option but to raise support. **The only way to broaden your support-raising comfort zone is to start raising support!** No amount of thinking about it, or even praying about it, will give you the experience you need to build your trust that God really does care, understand and stand with you in the process.

When the Children of Israel left Egypt, they almost immediately faced a comfort zone issue – the Red Sea. With the seemingly uncrossable sea looming large in front of them and the seemingly unbeatable army charging up behind them, their immediate response was to stop and question both God and Moses. The Living Bible paraphrases God's reply to Moses: *Tell the people to stop praying and start moving!* [EXODUS 14:15].

There are times when you already know the way forward, but you also know that it will make you uncomfortable. It doesn't help a lot to start questioning God and others he has involved in leading you this far. **It is time to start moving.** The Children of Israel had to trust God's leadership and guidance to cross a sea. Your task is tame by comparison. All you have to do is trust God's leading and guidance as you raise your support. But there comes a time when you have to start moving, dip your toes in the water (metaphorically speaking!) and see what God does.

My mother had an old saying from her childhood days on a farm – *you'll never plough a furrow in your mind.* **You'll never raise support by just thinking about it.** Also, you are guaranteed that whatever area of Christian ministry you work in you will find yourself dumped well beyond your comfort zone in some way or another. What better time to learn how to deal with this than right at the start, as you raise your support.

"I'm too scared to do it"

A nervousness that drives you into the arms of the Holy Spirit is fine. A fear that paralyses is a different matter. There is a disease that often inflicts people when raising support. It is 'dialitis' – the paralysis of the finger anywhere near a telephone dial! When you eventually get your dialitis controlled to the level that at least the finger can move, you call the potential supporter, hoping their line is engaged. You let it ring twice and slam down the phone, assuming they must be out. They get to the phone just as you hang up, hit 1471 and call you back. You stutter something about it not mattering that much and by the time you've finished, they have no idea what you're talking about.

If fear gets a hold of you to the extent that it prevents you talking to your friends and other contacts about what God has called you to and asking them if they'd like to be part of it, you need to deal with it. This is a spiritual battle. Get some friends to pray specifically for your fears. **Remember, it is the power of God's Holy Spirit working in you that will overcome your fears**, but the only way you'll know how you are doing is to test it. Don't wait until you **feel** that the fears have all gone. Satan is an expert at manipulating your feelings. And it may well be a progressive process anyway, with your fears disappearing into the

(See Chapter 24 – Establishing a Prayer Team)

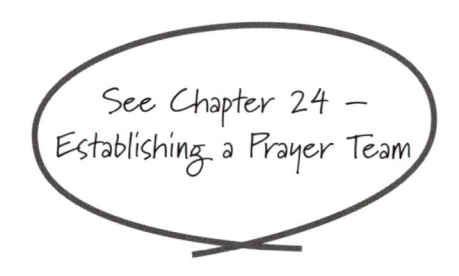

background as you take step after step in contacting people. It's wise to contact your good friends first, people you can be very open with about your fears, and ask them not only for support, but to critique your approach. Their honest appraisal of you will help build the confidence for the times you'll be contacting people you don't know so well.

"I don't like feeling dependent on other people"

Another of the spiritual battles that needs to be fought during support-raising is pride. We live in a society that values independence highly. In particular, the economic philosophy of the 1980s has fashioned the mindset of the generation that is currently exploring careers in Christian ministry: *"Get the best education you can, the best job that you can, the best home you can, become a stakeholder in society, you deserve it."*

For earlier generations, who had their values formed by the instability of the depression and the Second World War, the philosophy of *"live in rags before you run in debt"* dominated their economic agenda. Either way, the result is a western society where making it on your own, without help from others, is seen as a positive value.

Raising support challenges this. It upholds interdependence rather than independence. It encourages both the giver and the receiver to recognise that each is incomplete without the other; that each needs the other if both are to fulfil the roles to which God has called them. Like any family, the family of God works best when each member does their bit to the best of their ability. None of us can do God's work on our own. **Whether we are the givers or the receivers, we each need each other for us to be able to play our part to the full.**

"I don't have enough time"

Developing and maintaining your support team is likely to take more time than you think, especially if you want to build a team for the long term. I am constantly amazed, and equally disappointed, at the number of Christian organisations who ask their staff to raise support without allowing them the time that they need to work on it. **Raising support isn't just something you do to allow you to do your job. It is, in itself, an integral part of your job.** You are giving your time, prayers and abilities to whatever aspect of God's Kingdom's work he has called you to. You are building a team of people who will give their money, prayers and encouragement towards the same task. Any way you look at it, that's part of the job and it deserves an appropriate place in your priorities. It shouldn't be banished to your spare time and it shouldn't be shelved until you find a less hectic week.

I had just finished an initial two-day seminar on support training with a Christian organisation that had decided that they needed to give more of a focus to support-raising. At the end, one of the leaders announced that over the coming months the organisation was giving all their staff time off to work on their support. With the freedom that comes from being an outsider, I immediately, and publicly, objected. *"You don't give staff time off to do their job,"* I said. *"Yes,"* they said, *"but you know what we mean."* Well, no, I didn't. Would they have said that they were giving their staff time **off** to do evangelism or to do any other aspect of their normal work? No.

The underlying problem was that, in spite of all that was said, the leadership still didn't view raising support as something that was part of the job. It was an added extra, something that got you the money to do your job. Something to be fitted in when the real work was done. This is a disservice to the staff members and an insult to the role of the supporter. Certainly, Jesus seemed to consider his supporters to be more than external funders, to be kept informed with a few *'Dear Friends'* letters each year.

☞ **Take time.** Time to visit people, to write to them, to call them, to involve them as far as they are willing and able. Don't just squeeze your focus on support into a few spare minutes; give the process the time it deserves. Your initial support-raising can be quite intensive, almost a full-time job in itself. But even after your support is up to its target, spending up to ten per cent of your working time on maintaining your support is a good rule of thumb to work towards. Seems excessive? Not when you realise that it secures the money, prayers and encouragement you need to sustain the other 90 per cent.

"I don't know how"

For most people, effective support-raising is a learned skill. While you probably already have all the basic skills you need to raise your support, you may not have used them in this context before. You might also need to sharpen some skills that you've only used casually before, but now need to depend on to a much more significant extent. Like any skill development, it takes training as well as time. Each person raising support is different and each person giving support is different, so by training I don't mean learning a prepared script that can be turned on and off like a double-glazing sales pitch.

What I mean is learning enough about the Biblical principles of giving and receiving, the philosophy of why and how people give and some basic practices that will help you move forward. ☞ **Going through this workbook will help, but you should also check to see if there are any training courses available.** If your own organisation doesn't have some good training already available, look around. Check with Global Connections or Stewardship to see what they can recommend. It is also a good idea to find someone who has raised support and who has a positive attitude to it. Sit down with them, ask their advice, learn from them, ask them to mentor you.

(See pages 273-274)

When you've done all this, you still haven't learned how to raise and maintain your support. You will only learn this as you do it, developing a style that fits your circumstances and personality.

"I feel I'm being too pushy"

"I've left them with all the forms they need; they can fill it all in and post it to the office. They were at the meeting where I spoke about my work so they know that I need support; if they're interested, they'll get back to me."

We use every excuse we can think of to turn what should be an active process into a passive one. Isn't it strange that people who raise support often talk in terms of, *"we have to raise support"*? *Have to* is a negative term, implying something that is uncomfortable, that you don't look forward to, that you're only doing because you 'have to'. Ask the givers how they feel. They're doing fine, enjoying all the benefits we looked at earlier – getting blessed by God, having their needs met and their account with God credited. Even if they couldn't articulate their experiences in those terms, they certainly don't view their support for you as something that is uncomfortable, that they don't look forward to, that they're only doing because they *'have to'*.

So who has the problem?

> Chris and Jenny, who we didn't really know that well, sent us two gifts over the period of a few months, the first for £50, the second for £70. They weren't a couple who we would have automatically considered asking for support, but two gifts in such a short space of time convinced us otherwise. Having already thanked them for their gifts, I phoned and asked if they would like to support us on a monthly basis. Yes, they would be glad to talk about it.
>
> I was working with a Christian organisation in their area the following Thursday and arranged to have supper with them.
>
> During the evening, as arranged, I explained more about our work and how our support system operated and gave them a standing order form and Gift Aid declaration. They decided in principle that they would like to support us but, as is often the case, needed some more time to consider how much they would give and said they'd get back to me. I asked when they might be able to get back to me. Chris said they'd call over the weekend.
>
> Now I've been around long enough to recognise that something like my support isn't going to stay uppermost in their minds for three days, so I said that if they weren't able to get me over the

weekend, was it OK if I called them on Monday evening. Yes, it would be fine, but they'd call me over the weekend.

They didn't. Immediately my mind went into negative overdrive. Maybe they didn't mean it; maybe I had offended them in some way; maybe something happened to put them off. Of course I knew these weren't true. They'd already shown interest, they'd agreed to meet to talk about support and had enthusiastically agreed that they wanted to support us. But with two young children as well as the rest of their lives to live, our support slipped down their priority list between Thursday and Sunday.

Even though I've raised support for over 30 years, I still get nervous, so with a little apprehension I called. Chris was out and Jenny apologised; they hadn't had a chance to talk about our support. Could they call me back? Given that I was going to be back in their area the next Thursday I suggested that I call round again and finalise the details. Yes, that would be great.

Sure enough, the following Thursday evening they signed a standing order form for £50 a month.

It was only then that the other side of the story emerged. Chris and Jenny had set this £50 a month aside for another couple who had approached them several weeks before I did. Except this couple didn't have the forms with them. Instead they suggested that if Chris and Jenny were interested they could call their mission office to get the forms. (First mistake - always have support forms with you. You never know who you might bump into!)

With both Chris and Jenny working, where would they get the time to call a mission office? Eventually they got round to it... but the forms were never sent. What confused them even more, however, was that the other couple never got back in touch, not even to see if the forms had arrived. Put off by their experiences, they decided to give us the support instead. Jenny even said, with a touch of frustration, "Why do people make it so difficult for us to give them money!"

What Chris and Jenny didn't know was that I knew the other couple. A few weeks later I met them and relayed the supporters' side of the story. Their side of the story was simple. They had given Chris and Jenny all the information they needed to begin supporting them. To have pursued it any further would have left them feeling uncomfortable; they thought it would be too pushy. But who was left feeling uncomfortable as a result? Chris and Jenny.

"Why do people make it so difficult for us to give them money!"

There is a big lesson here. **Discomfort doesn't dissipate; it transfers.** If you're not prepared to live with a certain level of discomfort as you contact people, making it clear what you are planning to do, why you would like them to be part of your support team, what this would involve and who does what next in the process, they are the ones who will be left uncomfortable, unsure what you expect of them, unsure what they are supposed to do and, eventually, even guilty or annoyed that somehow their joy of giving has been robbed from them. ☞ **Do your supporters a favour: take the discomfort yourself. It's an occupational hazard.**

The story has a happy ending. After a number of attempts, Chris and Jenny got the forms and began supporting the other couple too. But it was hard work getting it set up. In the end Chris' and Jenny's persistence was as much to deal with their own feelings of frustration and annoyance as anything else. It could have been a lot easier all round three years earlier if the couple raising the support had kept some of the initiative themselves.

☞ **Don't confuse keeping the initiative with being pushy. They are different. It is very important to keep the initiative, both for your sake and for the supporter's.**

Notes

CHAPTER 7

WHAT CAN MAKE POTENTIAL SUPPORTERS FEEL UNCOMFORTABLE

As we've seen, discomfort in the process of support-raising doesn't just disappear because the person raising support chooses to walk away from it. It can often transfer to the person being asked to consider giving the support. Here are a few ways that the person being asked for support can end up feeling outside their comfort zone. Acting on some of these may well leave you feeling a bit uncomfortable. But sometimes it is a choice of you or them, and it's always better if **you** choose to take the discomfort.

"They're so busy with their lives, they're not interested in mine"

The person raising support tends to live, eat, sleep and breathe whatever it is God has called them to. This is especially true at the outset of a person's full-time involvement in Christian ministry, when they are taking a whole new direction in life, maybe even leaving their home country. Even for those who have been involved in Christian ministry for some years, there is a temptation to communicate from their own context and agenda.

However, the person being approached for support has their own life, their own job, their own family concerns, their own dreams, their own commitments. As the person raising support, you need to think with their mind, making connections between what God has called you to do and the context in which God has placed them. For example, if you are raising support to work with a youth organisation, ☞ **ask them how they find youth activities in their church,** or how their children are responding to the pressures of teenage years. Or ask what interests they already have in mission work.

In most cases, you will have a genuine interest in their lives. **Don't let the excitement of your calling dominate in a way that leaves the potential supporter feel that you have no interest in what God is doing in their lives.**

Think. ☞ **What do you know about the person you are encouraging to support you?** What are their interests? What is their home like? Is it very 'proper' or does it have a 'lived in' feel? By trying to think with the mind of the potential supporter, it is much easier to ensure that you allow them the comfort of talking about your work within the context of their lives.

But beware. If you're only going through the motions of seeming interested to stand a better chance of getting their money, then you need to back off. Remember, this isn't about getting money, it is about building a team of people who will express varying degrees of partnership with you in whatever it is God has called you to. If you don't have a genuine interest in the person you are approaching for support, then it is time you took stock of your own motivations before God.

"I've been treated like an audience, not a person"

I was leading a support seminar for the staff of a number of different missions and we had got to the fun bit – role-plays. One couple, on their way to work with a mission in Indonesia, volunteered to play the part of the couple raising support and another couple volunteered to be their friends whom they were planning to ask for support. After enough briefing for the couple playing the part of the potential supporters to act out their role as realistically as possible, the role-play started. The missionary couple were well organised, even to the point of having brought with them a well-prepared script that they took turns presenting.

The couple doing the asking barely drew breath between them as they charged through their script. Even the questions they had prepared as part of their script seemed calculated to expose the ignorance of the potential supporters rather than inform them, especially the way they were asked. ("*Do you know how many islands in Indonesia have no effective Christian witness? No? Well it's thousands!*") I sat thinking, "*How do I tell this keen couple, eager to do God's will, that this was about the worst support role-play I've ever seen?*" In the end I did what any self-respecting seminar leader would do – I asked others for their comments!

After a few moments of awkward silence, the wife of the couple playing the role of the potential supporter said, *"I feel like I've been run over by a juggernaut!"* The glazed look in both her and her husband's eyes confirmed the comment. Even in the role-play they felt uncomfortable.

In their desire to get it right, this young couple had scripted themselves to the nth degree. They dared not leave space for the potential supporter to draw them off on a tangent with questions or comments, so they simply kept total control of the presentation. Given that they were a quiet, unassuming couple, it made their out-of-character presentation all the more excruciatingly painful to watch. All they were trying to do was to get it right. But instead of engaging in a focused dialogue about their work and their need for support, they ended up with a domineering monologue.

During the next break, I sat with the couple to see how they could improve their presentation. They were still focused on their script and asked how they could improve it. I did the only thing that I thought would improve it – I tore it up! We then talked through how to share from their heart, involving the potential supporter in the discussion.

After the break, we repeated the role-play. Although the couple initially felt very insecure without their crutch, they slowly began displaying a passion that was missing in the scripted version. And they got good feedback from the 'pretend' support couple, who at last felt that they were engaging in a conversation with a purpose and a direction, not simply being hauled through a bad sales pitch.

☞ Remember, you are building a support team. Those joining the team need the chance to explore what is involved, both for them and for you, in this decision. And you need to be sure that you have communicated what you think you have communicated. A good focused conversation, where you know what you want to say, is only enhanced by good interaction as you go. Later in the book we will look in more depth at some ways of achieving this.

"I feel I'm only allowed to say 'yes'"

You know the feeling. Someone asks you if you could do them a favour. It's really quite inconvenient, but the way they have asked you gives you no option to say no. It is an uncomfortable feeling.

Support-raising should be like a room with two doors, one marked 'Yes' and one marked 'No'. Naturally, you encourage the person to choose the 'Yes' door (it would be a bit strange if you didn't!) but the person you are asking knows that they can choose the 'No' door. So what makes a person feel that there is only a 'Yes' door?

Sometimes you will find yourself being hesitant or apologetic in your approach because you don't want to appear to put undue pressure on people to support you. Far from taking pressure off people, this type of approach can make people feel that they have no option but to support you.

Picture it. Just before the Sunday morning service starts, someone asks you for a lift home from church. Normally you'd be delighted to offer them a lift, but this Sunday you had hoped to leave straight after the service to make sure you're home in time for the start of the Grand Prix. You're feeling just slightly guilty that you'll have to rush off without even waiting around for coffee – it is the last race of the Formula One season and the championship has come right down to the wire. You've also invited a couple of guys from work to join you – you've even convinced yourself that it's really an outreach opportunity! You're going to be very tight for time so you've already decided to leave during the last hymn to make a quick getaway – and giving him a lift will mean missing the start and the all-important first corner. But the way he asks puts you in a different type of corner! *"I know it's a bit out of your way, and I'm sure I could find somebody else, but is there any chance that you could give me a lift home after the service? If you've other plans and you can't do it, it's OK. I don't want to be any bother or anything."*

Now you know the story of the Good Samaritan, especially the bit about the two people too busy to help a person in need. You feel guilty saying no – after all, surely giving someone a lift home is a worthier thing to do than watching a motor race, however keen a fan you are and however good the friends are you'll be watching it with.

Ironically, the asker thinks that by offering you so many get-out clauses, they are making it easier for you to say no. But the reverse is true. The more a person hesitates and apologises in the way they ask, the more difficult it is to say no. In the case of the person needing a lift, if they had simply asked, *"Any chance of a lift home after the service?"* it would have been much easier to say, *"Normally I'd love to, but I'd planned to leave the service early today. I've a couple of guys coming from work to watch the Grand Prix with me and I want to make sure I'm there when they arrive. Have you tried Jim? He sometimes goes your way to pick up his mother-in-law on Sundays."*

☞ **Make sure that you don't put potential supporters in the uncomfortable position of feeling that they have to say 'yes'** because of the hesitant and semi-apologetic way you ask. A support relationship that begins with the supporter feeling sorry for you isn't a good foundation on which to build a lifetime of partnership.

Another way a person can feel pressured into the discomfort of saying 'yes', is when the asker is so overpowering, and their cause so apparently crucial, that to say 'no' would fly in the face of the momentum built up by the request. It's just easier to say 'yes' to get it over with!

☞ **Watch that you don't corner the person into feeling that they have no option but to say 'yes' by either the apologetic hesitation or the overwhelming exuberance of your ask.**

"I don't really understand what they're talking about"

People who live in 'Missionworld' speak a strange language. Long before texting came of age, Christian organisations and mission agencies had perfected the art of using initials and abbreviations to communicate. Just look at how so many groups are popularly known – YWAM, OM, SIM, OMF, SU, AIM, UFM, UCB… the list goes on. And when they aren't speaking in initials and abbreviations, they are using terms that only the true insider understands.

Whether it is the name of the organisation itself, a newly-developed strategy, a job title, a department name or some other aspect of Missionworld, you can be assured that the outside observer can be easily bemused by internal jargon. Recently a staff member in one of the groups I work with told me they were 82 per cent towards their SQW. The next day, with another group, one of their staff assured me that HRC was just about fully operational. In both cases I think I was supposed to be both pleased and impressed, but I'm not sure.

Because you live in Missionworld, you will, of necessity, use jargon terms to communicate internally. But those you will approach for support are outsiders, probably not that interested in your organisation or even in your work, but keenly interested in you. To communicate to them, ☞ **use real words, words that they understand**. If you really have to use an insider term, make sure that you explain it.

If you have ever been in a country where you don't know the local language very well, you know the discomfort of trying to understand what's happening around you. **Don't put your potential supporters through the same discomfort by speaking a language they don't know and may be too embarrassed to keep asking you to explain.**

"I'm not sure I know enough"

Each potential supporter needs different information in order to make an informed decision to support you. Your good friends, who know you well and trust you, really don't need to know that much. But it is most likely that you will need to approach people well outside your inner group of very close friends to reach your support target. These people may not know the background to why you have chosen the direction in your life that you have. They may not know much about the group you are planning to work with nor the needs the group is addressing. Even if you've sent them a prayer letter or two (or many more), don't assume that they have read them.

You live the information daily – it is part and parcel of your waking hours. They don't. If you expect them by some strange process of osmosis to be fully aware of all the background to your work, you will be disappointed and they will feel uncomfortable.

You may assume that the person is as aware as you are of information that you have built up over a period of weeks and months. But why should they be? ☞ **Use clarification questions** to make sure that the person you are asking to consider supporting you is as informed as they need to be to make the choice. Being asked to make a choice without the necessary information can be confusing and uncomfortable. It's like someone you may not know that well asking you, *"Do you want to go?"* You'd want to know where you are being asked to go, when you are supposed to leave, why you are being asked to go and how long you are likely to be gone.

Even if you do make sure you give your potential supporter all the information they need about your organisation as clearly as you possibly can, be warned that it still might not work. I have changed and disguised some of the details in this story to spare the blushes of all concerned.

> Colin worked for Neil, a Christian accountant who gave financial advice to a number of Christian organisations. Although he enjoyed his work, Colin felt that it was time for a change and joined ABC mission to work in their office. Not only was ABC one of Neil's clients, Neil also had high regard for their work and had helped them out in a number of ways in the past. He was more than happy to agree to support Colin in his new work, promising to send a good-sized cheque every six months. Sure enough, the first cheque arrived in ABC office... made out to CBA, a totally different organisation!

The moral of the story? Even your most informed supporters will still get it wrong sometimes. Don't assume anything and you won't be disappointed! Assume too much and you will – and your supporters will be bewildered in the process.

"I understand what you do every day, but what does your ministry achieve?"

The fact that you live in the middle of your daily ministry activities, or are planning to do so, means that it is easy to get caught up in the **process** of what you do rather than the end **product** of your work – the person whose life is touched by God's love in some way as a direct or indirect result of your work.

My guess is that, however your support gets to you, most of it will be spent on your basic living costs – housing, groceries, utilities, car expenses, etc. Given that most supporters have to cope with paying the same expenses for themselves, why should paying for your expenses excite them?

The answer isn't in the work that you do each day, it lies in the eventual **outcome** of the work that you do – there's a big difference between the two. The work that you do might not be that exciting every day. Much of it might be very routine, perhaps even veering towards the downright boring from time to time. But everything that you do is, in some way or another, working towards somebody somewhere hearing, seeing or in some other way experiencing God's love.

Some years ago, Mission Aviation Fellowship (MAF) did a survey of their supporters and found that a high percentage were not interested in flying. That's a problem for a mission whose main activity is flying people around! What the supporters were interested in were those whose lives were helped because MAF was able to fly someone into a difficult area where there were people in need. That's why, when you look at the MAF magazine, you are likely to read more stories about the impact of the work of doctors and evangelists than about pilots and aircraft engineers. And you'll notice in the photos, the person who has been helped by whoever MAF has flown into the area of need is prominent, with the plane sitting away in the background.

Yes, MAF flies people – it's what they do. But they only do it because there are people who have needs that can best be met by MAF flying in specialists with the gifts and skills to meet those needs. It takes a wise person (or organisation) to recognise that supporters are more interested in the outcome of their work than the detail of it.

Yes, there will always be people who show a keen interest in some obscure aspect of your work, but you need to be able to explain what you do in terms of the person who ultimately benefits from your work, no matter how indirect that impact seems to you.

Most supporters enjoy supporting people they know. They also enjoy knowing that their support is making a real difference in the life of somebody, somewhere. Very few enjoy simply funding a process, even if their good friend is involved.

☞ **Learn the stories of the eventual outcome of the work done by your organisation or cause, the lives touched and changed by God's love. This is what will encourage and excite the supporter, not necessarily all the detail of what you do with your time and their money.**

"I'm not sure how much I'm being asked to give"

> The head of a UK mission was visiting a businessman to ask him for a gift towards a new project the mission was launching. The two men didn't know each other, but a mutual friend, who was already supporting the mission, had suggested the contact and the businessman had agreed. Right at the outset of the conversation, the businessman said, "I am fed up with Christian organisations asking for my support, but leaving me to guess what they want me to do. Tell me why your project is important, how people will benefit as a result of the project, what it will cost, how much you already have been given towards it and how much you want me to give. Then I'll tell you if I'll give that amount."

This businessman was expressing, in a blunt way, what many potential supporters feel. **They don't feel comfortable guessing what you expect of them.** Most giving today is done out of surplus, not really sacrificially. It is unlikely that very many people will choose to downsize their lifestyle so that they can give you money. We live in an affluent society, with more money than we really need, so your supporters need help to know how much they should choose to give.

Your commitment to Christian ministry is a serious one. You are building a support team of people who you hope will take your work seriously as well. At the outset, some will be more interested than others and some will have greater giving ability than others. In one sense, it doesn't matter what you need, it matters more what they are willing and able to give.

I am not an advocate of always asking people whom I'm approaching for regular support to give specific amounts, although I know people who do and it works for them. What I would encourage, however, is ☞ **giving some sort of guidelines or ranges that the potential supporter can relate to**. For example, if you are right at the outset of your support-raising it can help to say something like: *"Whatever you can give will be great. If it helps, I'm looking for three or four people who can give £75–£100 per month, about six to ten who can give £50–£75 per month and ten to twenty who can give £25–£50 per month."*

Once your initial support is raised and you are approaching someone with an average or above average giving ability, then you could say something like, *"Whatever you can give will be great. If it helps, my current average support is about £35 per month and I've support from people up to £100 per month."* For those with possibly below average giving ability, simply change it to, *"…my current average support is about £35 per month and I've support from people from £7 per month".* By couching your request in these terms, you are not insisting that they give any one of the amounts, but simply giving some guidelines that help them make their own choice.

If you don't give some help to people, they are likely to give less than they could. They don't want to appear to be at the top of your support team (that could appear to be too presumptuous), so they settle for less. By showing them what the options are, they can be much more comfortable choosing an amount that they are more than willing to give and that will be a great help to you.

The more you know about the potential supporter and their interests, the more specific you can be, avoiding the embarrassment of either asking someone for an amount or range that is clearly beyond their ability or interest or the equal embarrassment of asking for so low a commitment that the person doesn't treat your ministry with the seriousness it deserves. In most cases, the temptation is to under-challenge rather than over-challenge. More on this later in the workbook.

☞ **Beware, too, of the 'Dear Friends' approach**: the newsletter asking for support in which it says something like, *"If everybody who receives this letter could just give £10 per month, then our support would be fully raised."* If you've been working through this book from the beginning, I would hope that you could spot a good number of wrong directions in this type of support-raising. One major flaw is that it assumes uniformity in giving ability and interest. What if I am really interested, but am struggling to make ends meet on a state pension? Maybe I can only afford £5 per month. Your request for £10 has priced me out of your support team. And what if I'm really interested and can easily give £100 per month? You have cheapened your ministry in my eyes by 90 per cent.

"I don't know what I need to do next"

Just imagine it. You've talked to someone about your work and they're really excited about what you're planning to do. Yes, they'd love to support you. But you don't have the standing order and Gift Aid forms with you. You promise to get them the forms within the next few days, but of course the next few days are really busy, so a week goes past and then another week. By then you can't remember who it was you'd promised to get the forms to.

Meanwhile, the supporter's initial enthusiasm gets tempered by the busyness of their normal life. They haven't changed their mind about supporting you, but a couple of weeks on they're not thinking about your support as keenly as they were the evening you talked about it. And if they did stop to think about it, they'd be a bit confused about the forms. Were you to get the forms to them or were they to collect them from you? It's all a bit hazy by now. You may well have lost a potential supporter and they may well be feeing a niggling discomfort about the unfinished business.

☞ Make it easy on the supporter. Always, always, always have with you whatever the potential supporter needs to respond to whatever you are asking them to do. It makes it much more comfortable for them to be able to complete what they said they'd like to do.

"It's my responsibility to make sure this is followed up"

In many cases when you approach someone for support, they need some time to think and pray about it, perhaps talk it over with their spouse, maybe work out how much they can give. In these circumstances it might sound right to leave it up to the person being asked for support to take the next step. But it isn't fair on them.

For the short time when you were talking to them about your support, it was the number one priority in their lives. But it is unrealistic to expect the potential supporter to keep your agenda at the forefront of their mind for however long it takes for them to make their final decision, decide on an amount, fill in the forms and send them back to you.

That doesn't mean that they've changed their mind. But unless it becomes their number one priority again for ten minutes, they may not actually get round to completing the process. In the enthusiasm of the initial conversation, they are likely to say that they'll get back to you about the decision. It is helpful to clarify at that point when that might be and also to leave yourself an open door to contact them again.

> Look back again at the story on pages 105-106. Who do you need to re-contact today?

Letters

The same applies when writing to people asking if they would support you, perhaps a friend who now lives too far away to justify a personal visit (see later in the book for a sample letter). Adding a PS saying, *"I'll give you a call in a few days to get your thoughts on this"* not only makes it possible for you to follow up your letter, but it also makes it easier for the potential supporter by not loading on them the responsibility of having to make the running in the process.

A word of caution with letters though. It can take more time than you'd think to actually get hold of somebody by phone. Don't make the mistake a friend of ours once made of posting almost 70 letters to potential supporters at one time, each saying that he would be in touch by phone within a few days. It was only as the pile of letters plopped into the post box that he realised with horror that there was no way that he could keep his word. It took him an embarrassing several months to eventually get hold of everyone, by which time many of them had forgotten that he had even written to them about his support!

SUMMARY

As you get into your support-raising, you will begin to develop patterns that work for you, ways of explaining your ministry, certain phrases that seem to communicate well, ways of helping people visualise the needs your work will be addressing, etc.

While each person you approach is different, both in their personality and in their knowledge of and interest in you and your work, you will find some ways of communicating that cross these differences.

You will also learn to think with the mind of the supporter and alter how you communicate your ministry from person to person so that you are talking within their context rather than just from yours.

All this is positive and you should establish your own personal effective communication style, amending and building it as you go. Developing and honing these skills will also help you in many other aspects of your ministry in the years to come.

Notes

CHAPTER 8

A FEW NOTES OF CAUTION

Don't let the £ signs rule

When you find yourself with an introduction to a couple whose second car is a six-month-old C class Merc, and whose living room is as big as your entire flat, it is difficult not to see these potential supporters through the focus of £ signs. In spite of what our society says, a person's real worth is not determined by their wealth. Their worth is determined by how much God was prepared to pay for them – the cross. **Try to treat everyone as playing an equal role in God's family business: someone loved by God, equal with you before God and called by God to be involved in some aspect of his Kingdom's work.**

Ironically, this should free you up to ask those with more money to give more, not just because they are wealthy, but because you are asking people to give in proportion to the financial situation God has placed them in. Jesus had among his supporters Mary Magdalene and Joanna, wife of Chuza, manager of Herod's household. They covered quite a spread across the social and financial spectrum. He was sensitive to each according to their own needs and situation, even though one was likely to have had access to more money than the other.

Don't take your supporters for granted

No matter how used you get to raising support, be careful that you don't take your supporters, or potential supporters, for granted. The moment you begin thinking of them as just a source of money and not as true partners in your work, you are beginning to lose the plot.

No one has an obligation to give you money, and your supporters have any number of ways they could use whatever money they choose to give you. If someone chooses to support you, or to increase their existing support for you, then they must have more money available to them when they make that decision than they had previously, or they are choosing to give you money that they previously used for something else.

It is unlikely that you will take your support for granted at the outset of your support-raising, but I have met a number of long-term missionaries who seem to forget that supporters have finite resources and whose first response to a need is simply to raise more money, when they should also be looking at other creative ways of meeting the need.

Watch how you present your ministry

There are a number of potentially negative ways in which you may inadvertently present your ministry to individuals or groups.

Beg: *"I don't deserve it, but have pity on me"*

My guess is that you're not likely to stoop to these depths in your support raising. But look back at the example given on page 112 of the man asking for a lift after church.

The more hesitant and apologetic you are in your approach to potential supporters, the more those you ask are likely to feel that they have no option but to say 'yes'. You might get their money, but you might not get their heart commitment.

Assume: *"I expect you to give me money"*

Again, you are not likely to say this. But in the back recesses of your mind, the thought may be lurking there, in spite of yourself: *"I've been a member of this church for years. I've taught Sunday School, helped run the Youth Group. My parents have been in the church for decades. Of course the church will support me and I'd hope by at least as much as they give to others."*

We need to have some sort of a plan in mind when raising support, with approaches made initially to those we think are most likely to support us. We might even have some expectation about what particular people or groups may give. This is OK. The problem comes when we turn these expectations into assumptions and then get critical of those who don't match up to our assumptions. It's the sort of response where your mind says: *"The church say they can only give me £500 per year, but look what they're wasting on the new building plans."* Or: *"Fine friends they turned out to be. Giving me just £10 per month and yet jetting off to Florida this summer – again!"*

You may be surprised how quickly Satan can tempt you into a critical and judgemental attitude. Remember what Jesus said: *Do not judge, or you too will be judged. For in the same way as you judge others, you will be judged, and with the measure you use, it will be measured to you.* [MATTHEW 7:1-2] If you are confident that you have approached the person or group in the right spirit, and with all the necessary information, then let God fight the battles with those who choose not to respond to his promptings. After all, it's his money, not yours or theirs.

Crisis: *"If you don't give, I can't meet my needs and the needs of those God has called me to help"*

This is another statement that you're not likely to make directly, but that you might communicate indirectly. Yes, God has put a specific call on your life. Yes, you do feel it deeply, to the extent of giving up your career, or at least setting it aside for a while. But others, including your supporters, have their own burdens from God. Burdens that they may feel just as deeply, but that might not involve them making the career change that you're facing. While you need to be as positive and expressive about your plans and your need for support as your personality allows, don't overwhelm people. **Remember, you are building a support team, some of whom will stay with you for as long as you'll live on a support basis. You're not simply getting money to meet an immediate need.**

Every year, through seminars and training sessions, I'm in contact with several hundred people who raise support. So I end up getting a lot of newsletters. A few – and thankfully it is just a few – fall into the 'crisis' category. There's always some potentially urgent situation that the person thinks warrants me responding, often needing money now, today. I don't mind this sort of letter from mission agencies and Christian organisations whose mailing lists are too large for them to really treat me as an individual. But I do mind them from someone who could as easily pick up the phone, write me a personal note or an email. In most cases there isn't really a crisis. It is just that the person has got into a habit of communicating with a sense of emergency, thinking that it makes their ministry seem more important. What it is more likely to do is create a weariness and also make me question their effectiveness: surely some of these supposed and frequent crises could have been foreseen and avoided?

Of course, sometimes there really is a crisis. Some years ago our car engine exploded beyond repair. At the time I was on the road every day travelling throughout Northern Ireland. We didn't have enough spare cash for what was a totally unbudgeted emergency. I phoned or wrote to the supporters I thought would be most likely to want to help us get mobile again and, sure enough, by the end of the week we had a new set of wheels.

We didn't try to add our urgent need for a car as a news item tagged onto the end of a newsletter. It was simply a case of *"Help. Our car has died and we need to get another one this week. Can you help?"* No one seemed to be annoyed at the request, almost all helped in one way or another and most expressed their appreciation that we had asked them.

I could count on the fingers of one hand the number of times we've asked our supporters for emergency help in over 30 years. Because if we only cry 'wolf' when there really is a wolf, people take our urgent requests seriously.

Pride: *"My ministry deserves your support"*

I was at a mission conference some years ago, standing at the back with a friend who was also involved in mission. We were listening to a mission leader giving a report of his work. We both knew the man, and what we were hearing didn't exactly square with what we knew – it was close, but not the truth, the whole truth and nothing but the truth. My friend whispered, *"Isn't it strange that mission work is only glorious when you're writing a newsletter or speaking at a conference."* It seemed that that particular speaker thought that if he could make his ministry seem just a bit more exciting, make it seem a bit more important, then those listening would consider him more worthy of their support.

In theory, pride can have no place in the life of a Christian. After all, your very salvation is a totally undeserved gift from God. In practice, we all want to show that we can make it on our own, that we're a little better than others, that we have worth in ourselves. True, but only because any worth we have has been given to us by God through the cross.

It's a difficult balance, knowing what to share and how to share it. If we get our motivation sorted out first, recognising that all we are and have are dependent on God, then the rest will flow more easily.

Here are a few questions that might seem complicated, but aren't really.

Who owns your salvation? Whose is it?

- *Simple really, it belongs to God.*

Did he use others to get his salvation to you?

- *In the vast majority of cases, yes, others were involved in bringing God's salvation to us.*

Did you get God's salvation because you deserved it because of what you did or who you are, or did you get it as an act of God's grace?

- *Clearly it was an act of God's grace undeserved by us.*

Now let's put these questions in the context of your support.

Who owns your support? Whose is it?

- *Simple really, it belongs to God, as does all the wealth in the world.*

Does he use others to get his support to you?

- *Yes. Unless God drops it on your lap by some sort of direct heavenly parachute, others will be involved in bringing God's support to you.*

Do you get God's support because you deserve it because of what you do or who you are, or do you get it as an act of God's grace?

- *It is as much an act of God's grace as your salvation is. The moment that we think that we deserve our support, that our work somehow warrants it in and of itself, we undermine the very faith we say we represent. Somehow it's easier to accept forgiveness and eternal life as undeserved gifts from God than it is to accept £50 per month from a friend up the street on the same basis.*

SUMMARY

- Do I view prospective supporters as **donors, investors** or **partners**?
- Do I **manipulate** a person by the way I ask?
- Do I have a **valid** ministry?
- Do I believe that asking is a **privilege** that provides someone with a genuine opportunity to be involved in ministry?

CHAPTER 9

DO YOUR HOMEWORK

Like any task, raising support needs good preparation. In the next section we'll look in more detail at some practical ways that you can begin building a support team. But even before that, there is some homework that needs to be done. By paying attention to the points in this chapter, you will begin establishing a good foundation, both in your mind and your practice, that will stand you in good stead for the rest of your support-raising.

Know your organisation or cause

☞ **Learn about its history, what its purpose is, what it does and does not do.**

- How many staff are there?
- Where do they work?
- What have been the main turning points in its history? and so on.

You may never need all this information, but at least you will be comfortable with questions that might arise. If you are new to the organisation, find out some **people-stories** that illustrate the work it does. When Jesus was asked to explain a very complex issue (God's Kingdom), he used people-stories. We know them as parables. If this was a good enough approach for Jesus, then it should do for you too!

What makes your work distinctive?

Being distinctive isn't being better than others. It simply means that if God has called your organisation or cause into existence, it must be to fulfil some aspect of his purpose that isn't already being done. For some groups, their distinctiveness is a specific geographical focus. For others, it might be a particular type of ministry. In some cases an organisation's name helps: Youth for Christ, International Nepal Fellowship, Operation Mobilisation, Wycliffe Bible Translators, Latin Link, University and Colleges Christian Fellowship, Habitat for Humanity, Mission Aviation Fellowship all give a clue to what the group does, why it was established or where it works.

☞ **Find out what makes your work distinctive.** What would be missing in the work of God's Kingdom if your work wasn't there? It might be big and global. Frontiers, for example, say clearly that they only work in teams to plant churches among Muslim peoples. It's not that others don't do this too, but it is the only thing that Frontiers does – that's what makes them distinctive. Others might be much more local, like the Youth for Christ centre in the Midlands that was in contact with every child in their area aged between five and 16 every month through their schools work. They built on that in all aspects of their work, including their communication to their supporters.

☞ **Learn your distinctives and fly them at the top of your flagpole.** I don't mean that you should boast about them, but if I'm going to support you it helps if you can tell me what your work adds to the growth of God's Kingdom.

Quality of your material

Although in many cases there is still vast room for improvement, most Christian organisations these days have publicity material of reasonable quality. Brochures, magazines and appeal letters are much better presented and easier to read than they were a couple of decades ago. Some organisations even provide their staff with profile leaflets with a bio blurb of the staff member, a summary of what their work will be and details of how they can be supported. This is all great, and it gives the staff member a good supply of well-produced material that enhances approaches they make for support, especially to people who may not know them or their organisation that well.

The problem comes when the staff member produces something themselves. Maybe a support presentation folder, a leaflet about their work and even their regular newsletter. If there is too big a gap between the quality and style of what is produced by the organisation and what the individual staff member produces, it can create a credibility gap. These days, with many organisations having the logo and other design material available for their staff on disc or via a download, there really is no excuse for shoddy personal publicity material.

☞ **If you work on your own, spend a bit of time, thought and money working out how you want to communicate information about your ministry.**

- Don't pack your publicity material with end-to-end copy. White space is your friend!
- Words are only useful if they are read, and the more words there are on a page, the less chance of them being read.
- Photos always win over words, especially photos that illustrate the need you are addressing, and one easy-to-see photo beats three small ones where you have to squint to see the detail.

☞ **You take your work seriously. You want your supporters to take your work seriously. Don't spoil it with badly produced material photocopied slightly crooked with the toner running out! Yes, there comes a point where the flashiness of your material is out of proportion to the type of work you will be doing or the amount of money you are raising. But in my experience, most people are so far the other side of the line on this that they could double the quality and cost of the material they self-produce and still have room to improve.**

Know how much support you need

Organisations differ in how much support their staff raise and what this represents. Some ask their staff to raise all their salary and expenses and only pay out if the money is in. Others may ask their staff to raise 100 per cent but will still pay a set amount, irrespective of what comes in. Some ask their staff to raise a lower percentage, making up the difference with centrally raised funds. Some pool the support, spreading it out equally among all staff. Others ring-fence each staff member's support to be used only for that particular staff member. Some set aside a percentage of the support that comes in for you to cover some central administration costs, including all the hidden costs of you being on their staff – recruiting you, training you, supervising you, handling your receipting etc. Others cover these costs from central fundraising.

Whatever system your organisation uses, you need to respect it. You can lobby internally for change in the system but don't be critical to others of your own organisation. It doesn't honour God. The system your organisation has isn't perfect (none is), but it has been developed over the years by experienced and Godly leaders who want to ensure that you are free to do what God has called you to in the context of your organisation.

If you are working independently or with an organisation that has little or no input into how much you should be raising, don't get caught in a false spirituality trap that says that it is more spiritual to be poor than to have plenty. Paul told the Philippians that he knew both a life of poverty and of plenty, but he didn't seem to hold one in higher regard than the other. You have a responsibility before God to look after those he has entrusted to your care, even if that is just yourself.

> ☞ You have also been called by God to a particular aspect of his work. Don't underestimate what this will cost. It deserves as much time, prayers, manpower and money as you can recruit to the task. Don't short-change it – eternity is too important to miss an opportunity to bring God's love to someone just because you felt a bit uncomfortable raising the right amount of support.

Know your audience

We'll look at this in more depth later, but you should be thinking about who you will contact for support and why. It is a given that you will feel nervous, but don't let your nervousness be a limiting factor in those you'll contact. God has given you a network of contacts already. ☞ **Explore these in your mind and on paper.** Instead of allowing yourself to be convinced that none of your contacts will be interested in supporting you, turn this round. See if you can come up with reasons why different people you know might be interested.

So, instead of saying about your old Sunday School teacher, *"I can't contact her, I haven't seen her in about four years,"* you could try, *"I wonder what it would mean to my old Sunday School teacher to know that one of her class really did listen and that I'm now going to work with ABC mission?"*

It's easy to come up with reasons why not to contact people. It takes a bit more thought to come up with reasons why you should. In most cases, those you contact will be more than happy to consider supporting you. It is the asker who has the problem, not them.

Be alert to circumstances

The circumstances of the giver have more bearing on whether or not they support you than your circumstances do. While responses don't always follow what we anticipate, issues like someone losing their job, a newly-launched church building project or a couple whose triplet daughters have all announced their engagements may cause you to think about if and how someone should be approached.

Factors like these shouldn't mean that you don't approach someone at all. They may welcome the chance to help, even in a limited way, but they may cause you to add a cautionary note in your approach. Something like, *"I realise your finances will be stretched with Bertha, Martha and Agatha all getting married this year. But your prayers have helped me get this far, so I didn't want to bypass you. I'd be delighted if you could be part of my support team, at whatever level might work for you right now."*

If you choose not to approach people because you feel they might not be able to support you financially, the message you are in danger of giving out is that you're only interested in people with money. You know that's not true, but they might not. **At least let them say no themselves rather than you saying it for them.** And you might be surprised. One of our largest supporters is a couple who I would have thought had among the least giving ability of our friends. You never know!

Glass half-empty or half-full?

Be careful, however, that you don't read more into situations than you should. I was meeting with the staff of a UK-based organisation, helping each of them work out a support-raising plan. One was a woman in her mid-20s who was quite pessimistic about her support prospects. *"The problem with my situation"* she said, *"is that most of my friends are students or first earners. The students have no money and the first earners are in debt. There's no one I can ask for support."*

The very next staff member I met with was another woman in her mid-20s who was really looking forward to raising support. *"The great thing about my situation"* she said, *"is that most of my friends are either students or first earners. They mightn't have a lot of money, but no one has taught them about giving from what little they have. This is a great chance to help them get their giving sorted out before they get too trapped by materialism. I can't wait to get out there and sign them up."*

Two people facing the same set of circumstances. One was paralysed by what couldn't be done. The other saw it as an opportunity for discipleship. Any guesses which one did a better job on their support?

Right first time!

SECTION 3

MAKING IT WORK

CHAPTER 10

Getting Going

Now that we've looked at some Biblical principles of giving and receiving and also some of the hows and whys of giving, it's time to explore some practical pointers for raising support.

There is no magic formula that you can simply conjure up that will ensure your success. This is about building relationships and, no less than in any other aspect of life, your approach will differ in some ways from anyone else's. Your approach will also differ depending on who you are talking to. The style used to communicate to a 75-year-old lady in your church will be very different from the style you would use with a 24-year-old lad at work.

Remember also that you are wandering around a spiritual minefield as you raise support. When someone agrees to support you, there are at least three special benefits: they get blessed by God for their giving; you get personally encouraged that another person wants to join your team; the work of God's Kingdom gets enhanced as more financial resources are applied to the task. You can be sure that Satan will do all that he can to prevent any of this happening.

What about support from non-Christians?

This question crops up every time I lead a support seminar.

First of all, **there is no money that doesn't belong to God**. As we've already looked at earlier, Psalm 24:1 tells us: *The earth is the Lord's, and everything in it, the world, and all who live in it.* There may be God's money in the hands of ungodly people, but there are no resources on the earth that do not owe their existence to God.

It is good to start off from the perspective that all money is God's and the more that can be used to further his Kingdom, the better, whether given by Christians or non-Christians. Remember, Nehemiah used gifts from King Artaxerxes to rebuild Jerusalem.

But there are a few points to bear in mind when receiving support from non-Christians.

- They can give you money, but they can't pray for you. Money is only part of the overall support package. Prayer is another vital ingredient. With the best will in the world, those who do not have a personal relationship themselves with God will not be in a position to offer this spiritual fuel for your work. Be careful that you don't have too many supporters who can't also pray for you.

- Your non-Christian friends may have a problem with the church, but they probably have some concept of a loving God who wants good to happen to people. Whatever you are planning to do, it is probably closer to what they think the church **should** be doing than what they think it actually is doing. This is a great opportunity to put your faith right up the flagpole. Explain that this is faith in action, showing and telling God's love to people in need, whether that need is spiritual or physical. Help them see that this is the sort of thing that Christians have been doing from day one.

- You will need a different jargon. Terms like 'support', 'missionary' and 'ministry' are internal terms that make sense to those who are used to a Christian environment. In the charity world, different words are used: sponsorship, community worker, development project and so on. You will need to change how you explain your work and the financing of it in a way that your non-Christian friend can relate to.

- Recent surveys show that Christians give almost ten times more than non-Christians – and not just because they give to their churches. Even with church giving taken out of the equation, Christians give more than non-Christians to charitable causes. It makes sense. Giving is part of God's character, so the more a person's relationship with God matures, the more they should understand and practise God's principles of giving. How often do you hear non-Christians being encouraged to give away at least ten per cent of their income? Yet this is often taught to churches.

- It gives you a chance to talk more openly about your faith to your non-Christian supporters. They are paying you to show or tell God's love to others. It only makes sense for you to use the opportunity to talk to them about what you are doing and explain God's love to them also.

- Unless you have a real reason not to, include them in your normal communication after they have signed up, prayer letters and all. It will help them see that your work is not just social, but has a strong spiritual dimension to it, even if in some cases, the day-to-day activities may have more of a social or community focus.

So, yes, by all means get your non-Christian friends to sign up. They may have no one else who will talk to them about issues of faith, and they are paying you to do just that!

But, for the rest of this workbook, I'm assuming that you are raising support primarily from Christians and the suggestions and examples reflect this. You will need to adjust some of the ideas slightly to make them work for non-Christians.

Getting personal

I have already mentioned in the introduction that I've taken it as a given that you have surrounded yourself in prayer during this whole process. However, it is sometimes worth re-stating the obvious. ☞ **Make sure that you are constantly praying about all aspects of your support-raising and are also having others pray for you.**

In this section I will suggest an outline support-raising plan that I have found useful over the years, as have hundreds of others I've helped in many different organisations. It is intended as a basic template, with a particular focus on making personal appointments. To make it as clear and transferable as possible, I will use lots of detail and examples. These are not meant to be followed slavishly, but rather they are meant to give you some handles to hold on to as you build your own support-raising plan.

Because of the discomfort issues we looked at earlier, most people's default position when facing the challenge of raising support is to hide behind impersonal communication, whether it be asking (or at least hinting and hoping) in prayer letters or at public meetings. While these can be helpful ways of letting people know that there is a need, they are not the best ways, by a long stretch, of encouraging people to respond directly to the need.

They are the equivalent of the note in the church magazine, or in the Sunday morning announcements, that there is a need for a few more volunteers for the Sunday School and that anyone interested should see Mrs Jones after the service. Everybody hopes that somebody else will go to see Mrs Jones. They don't think that the announcement is for them. Even the few who might be interested in volunteering will get waylaid after the service (*"Just got to pop over to ask Jim how Mary's operation went"*) and they somehow won't find the time to get round to it. It would be much more effective if Mrs Jones asked people personally to volunteer. *"Sarah, would you like to try helping at the Sunday School? I've seen how you are with children and you'd be great. You could give it a try for a couple of months, two weeks on, two weeks off, to see how it goes."* Not only does Sarah know that Mrs Jones would like her in particular to help, but she also knows why. And she has some idea of what Mrs Jones is expecting of her. In this sort of scenario, Mrs Jones is much more likely to get the people she thinks would be best at the job rather than have to take the few who might surface from a broad, impersonal announcement.

Raising support is not very different. It is about encouraging a particular person, who you think might be interested in supporting you, to give serious consideration to joining your support team. **It is much better done over a cup of coffee than through a prayer letter.**

I'm assuming that you are at or near the start of your support-raising, possibly with a target to achieve that seems a bit daunting and that you have some time limit by which you hope, or need, to have your support raised. Or maybe you've been living on a support basis for some years, but you need to give your support some serious attention at this stage. In other words, this practical section assumes that you've moved beyond the luxury of theoretical reflection and are getting down to the reality of actually working on it.

(If this isn't the case for you and perhaps you are not in immediate need of new supporters, the principles should nevertheless still apply.)

In seminar settings we use interaction, worked examples and role-plays during this section. Role-plays can be fun, but they can also feel a bit false and awkward. And for the good reason that they are fun and also a bit false and awkward! But they are a good way of learning and beginning to put into practice some of the principles before you are let loose on the unsuspecting public.

> ☞ **There are times in this section of the book where in a seminar we would take a break to role-play what we've just been discussing. Find someone to work with you on this. Their feedback on how you did, whether they understood what you were asking them to consider, what jargon terms you used and so on will be a great help to you. Although it might feel strange and a bit unreal, let me assure you that it is better to sweat more during a role-play with a friend in order to make sure that you sweat less during the real thing!**

CHAPTER 11

HOW MANY FISH IN YOUR SEA?

The first step in the plan is to work out **the network of contacts that has God already given you.** Let me illustrate what I mean.

I enjoy fishing. It isn't by any means the greatest passion of my life, but we do try to take two weeks' holiday each September when we head off to the south Donegal coast, me with my fishing rods and Phyllis with a pile of books. In fact, my one claim to fame is that I taught Tony Blair to fish, right there in south Donegal, in the early 1960s. It's a long story that hasn't yet earned me a place in the New Year's honours list!

But back to fishing. There's a small pier that I enjoy fishing off and if I catch four or five fish in a couple of hours, I'm delighted. But I don't go to that pier because there are only four or five fish there. I go because I know that there are potentially hundreds of fish in that area. I just hope that a few of them might take a fancy to whatever bait I pass in front of them.

Working out your potential is equivalent to working out how many fish are in your sea. This isn't an exercise in trying to identify who might support you or who you should contact about support. It is simply trying to work out the extent of the relationships God has given you. We can work out later where would be a good place to start in terms of contacting people about supporting you, but that's further down the line.

For now, ☞ **take some time and list all the Christians you know or who know you.** There will probably be non-Christians who'll want to support you also, but for now let's concentrate on Christians. As well as supporting you financially, they can pray for you and get involved in other ways that have a direct spiritual impact on your work in ways that non-Christians can't do.

☞ **Don't be tempted to edit your list at this stage.** Just because you haven't seen the person for a few years or because you wouldn't really call them a good friend is no reason not to include them.

Remember, this isn't a list of people you'll contact for support, so feel free to ☞ **add as many names as you can think of**.

To help you get started, I've drawn up a list of categories (see below). They might not all apply to you and you may well be able to add other categories that I haven't thought of. But ☞ **start with this list and add as many names to each category as you can.** Don't add people just for the sake of it: *"The old man with grey hair who sits near the back of the church"* isn't good enough! It helps if you know at least their first or last name.

You'll notice that I've put family at the end of the list of categories. All our other contacts are, to some extent, relationships of choice. With family, we don't have much choice who we get! You may be part of a great Godly heritage where your family is very supportive of your decision to go into Christian ministry and would be delighted to support you. On the other hand, you might be the only Christian in your family and the rest of them think that you're completely crazy, making the biggest mistake of your life and they have no intention of doing anything to help you throw away whatever career you've had up to now. Or you may be somewhere in between. ☞ **Add family members to your list regardless.** You can work out later what might be the best approach to take with them on an individual basis.

The very exercise of drawing up your list will jog your memory and will dig up names from your past. Enjoy the exercise. This is a list of the Christian network God has placed you in. What a privilege to live in a society where we have the freedom to develop such a large group of Christian contacts!

> *If you end up with 100 names or fewer, you have probably left out names that you could have included. Go back to the list again, taking your blinkers off, and see how many others you can add.*

> **Note: Don't read beyond this point until you've drawn up your list!**

Use the page opposite or a sheet of paper to start compiling your list.

- friends
- current and former churches/pastors/Youth Groups/Sunday School and Bible class leaders
- those who have had a spiritual impact in your life
- those in whose life you have had a spiritual impact
- parents of those in whose life you have had a spiritual impact
- former employers/work-mates
- old school friends/teachers
- former college/university lecturers
- student friends
- dentist, doctor, solicitor, bank manager
- business men and women
- neighbours/former neighbours
- wedding list (if you're married!)
- youth club/youth organisation leaders
- address book (electronic and paper)
- parents' visitors' book
- your visitors' book
- Christmas card list
- close family and other relatives

How Many Fish in Your Sea?

Notes

Making it Work

CHAPTER 12

WHO TOPS YOUR LIST?

So how did you get on with your list? It should have given you a good base to build on. Remember, this isn't a list of potential supporters. It is just a snapshot of what your total network of Christian contacts looks like right now. Keep this list and add to it as more names come to your mind and also as you meet new people. Your network of contacts, like everyone's, is constantly changing.

Why would anyone on this list be interested in supporting you? What do any of them know about your decision to go into Christian ministry?

☞ Go back to *How do supporters decide to support you?* on page 73 and use the decision-making ladder to identify where each of those on your list is right now in their ability to make a decision about supporting you. ☞ **Number them 1–6**, 1 meaning not even aware that you are planning to work with a Christian organisation and 6 for those whose committed support has already started. Don't get bogged down in fine nuances of differences in this process. It isn't meant to be an exact science, so agonising for a couple of minutes about whether someone is a 3.8 or 4.2 isn't really going to be a good use of your time.

☞ **Take another look at your list now.** Who is at the top end of the *'knows a bit more and shows some interest'* category? Who did you put in the *'knows enough to make a decision'* and *'already decided'* categories? These are likely to be the best people to start with, while you look for opportunities to build a platform of awareness and interest among those at lower stages on the ladder.

But even if you do select out those who are likely to be most interested, there are probably still a lot of names on that list. **So where do you start?**

☞ Ask yourself, **"If God allowed me to have just one supporter, who would I want?"** The name that comes to your mind won't necessarily be the wealthiest person on your list. It will be the friend you've known for the longest time; or someone in your church who has been a special encouragement to you in your decision to go into

Christian ministry; or maybe a colleague in work whose witness has been a challenge to you in your own Christian life; or perhaps your church itself. If the person or group that springs to mind as the one supporter you'd really like to have on board with you also happens to have the ability to give a lot of money, happy days! But my guess is that you wouldn't select your one and only supporter based just on the amount they could give.

☞ **Go back to your list and circle the name you've just thought of.** What better place to start than with the person you'd most like to join you in the journey God has called you to?

> *What better place to start than with the person you'd most like to join you in the journey God has called you to?*

But you'll need more than one supporter. **So who would your next five be?** ☞ **Highlight their names as well.** Now you've got a good base to begin with.

As you begin working on your support, you'll find that it doesn't work out the way you had planned. Someone who you thought would be interested may, for whatever reason, not turn out to be as interested as you had thought. And you can be sure that people will appear apparently from nowhere who will end up among your most committed supporters. Some will show up at your door offering to support you. Others, who you felt sure would approach you themselves, might need more encouragement and reminders from you than you'd ever have expected in order to turn their interest into a firm commitment.

SUMMARY

However it works out in practice, you need to start somewhere. So having your first handful of 'those I most want' is as good a place to start as any.

CHAPTER 13

GET SORTED

Right from the start, get control and keep control.

Of what, you ask?

Of information and detail.

It's the morning after the night before, when you had spoken about your work and your need for support to a group in a friend's house. Your warm fuzzy feelings about the previous evening slowly turn into a cold sweat. You can't remember the names of the two couples (or was it one couple and one single?) who took standing order forms and said that they'd get back to you. And then there was the other person who said that they'd like to meet up for lunch some day to talk about your support. Was that the tall guy who had to leave soon after you'd finished, or was he the one with the cousin who used to work with the same group you're joining? If he was the one with the cousin, then who on earth did you arrange to have lunch with? And was it this Tuesday or next Tuesday?

No, you think. I wouldn't forget details like that.

Let me assure you (and this is from the depths of despairing personal experience in the past!) – you will.

> *A few months previously, Jim had agreed to support us. We had known each other a bit in the past, but he'd jumped at the chance to join our support team and was eager to introduce us to others who could support us also – especially his large extended family.*
>
> *So he and his wife Lorna hosted an evening in their house for all his brothers and sisters, along with an assortment of wives, husbands, fiancés and not-yet fiancés for us to explain about our work and to present our support needs.*
>
> *It was a great night, with a lot of interest among those present. One said that they had already decided to support us before they came; two others took forms and said that they'd get back to us; one asked us round to their house for supper the next*

week. The rest offered some signs of interest without any firm commitments. It was great!

Except that we had no idea who was who. They all knew who we were, but all we knew was that they were either one of Jim's siblings, or connected to one of his siblings. And they didn't help by not sitting with their respective partners, adding to our confusion. Yes, a few had introduced themselves by name, but in the confusion of the convivial atmosphere of what was, in effect, a happy family gathering, it all got a bit lost.

Realising that I was fast losing control of the information, as soon as they had all left I sat down with Jim and plied him with questions. "Who was the one with the beard and who was he married to?" "What was the name of the couple who had to leave early?" "Who was that wearing the red dress and was that her husband she was sitting beside?"

I didn't go to bed until I had sorted out **and written down** *all the information I needed to take the whole process forward in an appropriate way with each person.*

It was the night I realised how important it was to stay in control of the information. If I hadn't, can you imagine how I'd have felt, not to mention looked, in the days following that evening, contacting each of Jim's family, asking them to clarify if it was they who had agreed to support us or were they the ones who had invited us round for supper! We'd have been too embarrassed and simply wouldn't have done it. They would have been left feeling that we weren't really interested in them and we'd have been left without some fantastic supporters in the following years.

As you review your list, the names on it are likely to fall into one of the following three broad groupings:

- individuals you can visit
- individuals too far away to visit
- groups (churches etc).

☞ **From the outset, keep a record of everybody**, especially those you plan to contact. This will need to be in a format that you can carry with you at all times, that gives you an immediate overview of all the information and that can be easily updated. And no, you don't need a complicated database programme. The best option I have found is a **simple card-index file** which, in my opinion, beats the best PDA or laptop system for this purpose.

If you are working with any sort of intensity on your support, I strongly recommend that you follow the points below. Doing so will save you and, more importantly, your supporters from misunderstandings, confusion, embarrassment and incomplete loose ends. If you feel that you can adapt it to a pattern that suits you better, great. Just make sure that it gives you all the detail you need about each person, at each stage of the process.

☞ **Record the basic details of each person and group on your list**: name, address, phone numbers, email address, etc. If you haven't got all the information you need, record what you do have and try to fill in the missing bits as soon as you can. The best person to ask is usually the person themselves! Check any unusual spelling – is it Catherine or Kathryn, Steven or Stephen, Brown or Browne? I'm Myles with a y. If someone writes to me as Miles, it feels a bit strange, like I've got a letter from someone who doesn't really know me.

☞ **Sort the list into basic categories**: eg, appointments to be made; appointments set; contact again for decision; send thank you; letters to be written; letters awaiting reply; support started; prayer letter only; no further contact; groups to contact.

☞ **Re-classify your list as you contact people.** Keeping your file up to date all the time will help you to know exactly what you need to do next with each person.

☞ So, stop right now and go out and get a bundle of index cards, a box to put them in and a set of dividers. Take time over the next couple of days to begin recording as much detail as you have about those you think could be potential supporters. Make sure you include at least all the names that you listed in category 3 ('interested') or higher in the last exercise. And don't forget that your list needs to be dynamic, not static.

As you work on raising your support, you will meet new people every week, sometimes every day. Add them to your list and write a card for them, especially if they show any interest in you or your work.

Notes

CHAPTER 14

PEPPER MILLS AND BRIDESMAIDS

So how should you go about approaching people for support?

Let's take two other situations where you might choose to ask someone to do something for you.

Pepper mills

You are sitting at a table having a meal with some friends. The food is great, but you'd like just a bit more pepper. The problem is that the pepper mill is right at the other end of the table, beside the person you least know. What do you do? Try a vague comment that you hope will stimulate someone into action? *"This meal is great; just needs a hint more pepper!"* Or maybe try a general question, *"If anyone would be interested in passing me some pepper, perhaps they could let me know?"* Of course not. You simply catch the eye of the person at the end of the table and ask if they'd pass you the pepper. Or if you can't get their attention and you don't know them well enough to call across the table to them, then you ask someone further up the table who you do know, or whose eye you can catch, if they could ask the person at the top of the table to pass the pepper.

Is anyone annoyed at this direct approach? No. But then again, asking someone to pass a pepper mill to the other end of a table isn't really all that big a deal.

So let's look at another example.

And bridesmaids

You are planning to get married and you need a bridesmaid. (If you're a bloke, read 'best man' for 'bridesmaid' and please make similar adjustments for the rest of this example!) You've decided to have three bridesmaids and you know who your top three choices would be. What do you do? Send a *'Dear Friends'* letter to all your contacts telling them that you've got engaged and that you need a number of bridesmaids to make the wedding work properly and that if anyone would like to be one of your bridesmaids, do get in touch? And then pray like crazy that the three you'd really like are the first three to call you? Or maybe make an announcement in your church that you're getting married and saying that if God is leading anyone to be one of your bridesmaids, they should contact you after the service?

No, of course you wouldn't! You'd ask your top choices face to face if you could. If they lived too far away for you to see them, then you'd call them, email them or write them an excited note. You'd no doubt explain why you wanted them to be your bridesmaids, what would be involved and tell them how much you want them to be part of your special day.

This is one of the biggest events of your life, a lot more important than asking for the pepper! You want to get it as right as you can and you want the right people with you. You wouldn't risk jeopardising the day by simply throwing the information that you need bridesmaids into the wind and seeing what blows back.

So, back to the reality of raising support

Raising support has elements of both the "Would you pass the pepper?" and the "Would you be my bridesmaid?" scenarios.

Right now you need support and it is in the hands of other people, like the pepper mill. Some of these are people you know well and have a close relationship with; others you don't know that well and you may not have any significant relationship with them at all. A few of those you're close to may well take the initiative and approach you to offer support. Most others, like the person with the pepper mill, might need some help in recognising your need for support, maybe even an introduction from someone who knows both of you quite well.

And, like the bridesmaids, you want to get it right, not depending on a hint and hope method to surface those you'd really like to come with you on this important journey you're embarking on. **You want to make sure that those on your support team know why you want them to be your supporters, what being a supporter will involve and how they can be the best help to you in following God's call on your life.**

There's an added element to raising support that doesn't usually crop up when choosing bridesmaids. Sometimes your best and most committed supporters will come from those you didn't know before they decided to support you. I'm still not sure why this is, but I suspect that it is precisely because there is no history in your relationship. Their first connection with you is as someone involved in Christian ministry who they choose to support – and it grows from there.

From interest to involvement

As with getting the pepper or choosing a bridesmaid, the more personal the approach, the more positive the response. You are also more likely to get the right people on board; people who don't just give money but who also pray for you and encourage you.

Yes, you can gain people's **interest** with a more impersonal style of communication, but to make your support work you will need some way of helping people move from interest to **involvement**.

> **Involvement**
> ↑
> Personal visit
>   Handwritten letter with phone call
>   Email with phone call
>   Personalised word-processed letter followed by phone call
>   Personalised letter without phone call
>   General letter (Dear Friends)
>   Meeting
>   Newsletter
>   Personalised brochure
>   Organisation's general brochure
>   ↓
>   **Interest**

This chart gives an idea of the sliding scale of effectiveness with different methods of communication. To encourage a positive response of true involvement normally requires as personal an approach as the circumstances allow. **Right at the top of the effectiveness list is sitting down with a friend, over a cup of coffee, sharing what God has put on your heart and asking them if they'd like to be part of God's exciting plan for your life.**

The sliding scale of comfort

But the further up the effectiveness ladder you climb, the more uncomfortable it can be. There is no fear of rejection if you simply make an announcement in church or send out a general letter to everyone about your support. You don't know who was even listening in church or who actually read the letter! On the other hand, to sit down face to face with a friend and ask them if they'd like to join your support team – that's a different matter.

☞ **But look back again at Chapter 7.** What makes you uncomfortable can often leave the person you're asking feeling more at ease with the situation and, conversely, if you only communicate in a way that avoids you facing discomfort, it may well leave the other person feeling uncomfortable.

☞ So, build your plan around as much direct contact with people as possible. Yes, you may well need to use less personal types of communication to build awareness and interest among people. But don't expect to reap much of a support harvest from a 'throw it all in the air and see what lands' style of communication.

Steve and Johanna had worked overseas with Wycliffe Bible Translators for some years before they returned to the UK for Steve to take on a highly specialised technical role at Wycliffe's office near High Wycombe. Their support had never been great, but by then it had dropped to just over 60 per cent and Wycliffe helped them over the years by adding to their support from some general funds.

Because Wycliffe wanted them to stay, Steve and Johanna were allowed time to work on their support, with some general funds still added to their support until their support would get up to 100 per cent.

Steve and Johanna had gone overseas at a time when Wycliffe had operated a non-ask policy and this suited them well, as the thought of being more direct about their support-raising left them feeling uncomfortable.

In spite of their prayers and the odd mention about their support discreetly tucked away in a corner of their prayer letter, Steve and Johanna's support continued to slide until it reached a crisis point of 62 per cent.

In the meantime, Wycliffe had changed their policy so that they both allowed and encouraged their staff to be more open when informing and asking people about support. Steve and Johanna weren't very comfortable with this new direction, but they faced a quandary. If their support didn't improve, they would have to leave. However, given that all else had failed, if they were going to stay they faced the discomfort of becoming more direct in their asking.

They came within a whisker of resigning. But they knew in their hearts that God wanted them to stay.

So, with nothing else to lose, they decided to take a more direct approach.

Not only did they mention their support crisis much more prominently in their prayer letters, they contacted a few people personally by letter. (They still couldn't summon up the courage to contact people face to face.)

The husband of one couple they wrote to phoned and asked if he could come round to talk about the situation. They were delighted to have got a positive response and happily arranged a time for him to visit.

You can imagine their horror and embarrassment when he told them that he was facing the prospect of redundancy. In their eagerness to find their support, they had offended someone they didn't really know very well by asking for money right at the time he was least able to give it. Swift apologies flowed.

"No," he responded, "it's not that; you weren't to know about my job situation. The reason I wanted to see you is that from your letter it's clear that your job with Wycliffe is under threat for financial reasons. My job is also under threat for financial reasons. The difference is that I'm really not coping well with this, not handling it in a Godly way. You, on the other hand, are handling your situation from a faith perspective. There's no one else I can turn to who understands. Will you help me get a faith perspective on my situation?"

For well over an hour they prayed with him, shared scriptures together and generally helped him get his eyes off his circumstances and back onto God. He wept as they talked, relieved to find someone who could understand and help him. He left with a much more Godly perspective than he had brought.

As I write this, I've just heard that Steve and Johanna have reached their 100 per cent support target. But even more importantly, they have a totally different understanding of the support process itself. "Never in our wildest dreams," they wrote, "could we have ever imagined being able to give so much to someone else by asking them to consider giving support to us!"

CHAPTER 15

Taking the Plunge

You've got your list, set up a fail-safe system for keeping records as you go, and you've identified the top half-dozen people who you'd like to be on your support team.

You're sufficiently convinced that a personal approach is the best way forward for you to give it a try, in spite of your own discomfort. So what next?

As I've already said, there is no one-size-fits-all magic template that will ensure success on every occasion. But this chapter and the next give some basic guidelines that will help you become more confident as you approach people. Use these guidelines in a way that suits you best and, more importantly, apply them in a way that is best for each potential supporter you approach.

These guidelines aren't rocket science. In fact, you probably follow them automatically in a whole range of ways in other aspects of your life. It's simply asking someone to help out with something you're involved in. Yes, asking someone to support you financially might be a bit more significant than asking someone to give you a hand decorating your living room, but the same principles apply.

1. Choose someone to contact
2. Set up a time to meet them
3. Meet them
4. Thank them
5. Follow-up

In this chapter we'll look at the first two stages of this process – getting from first thinking about it to arranging to meet someone to talk about your work and support needs.

In the next chapter we'll look at what you do when you meet with a potential supporter and what happens afterwards.

Choose someone to contact

This may well be one of the half-dozen people you've already marked on your list as those you'd really like on your support team. If not, it should certainly be someone who has already shown interest in your ministry, or someone who you think should be interested, based on your relationship with them. It's always good to start off with a likely winner!

Set up a time to meet

Even if it's someone you might bump into at church, at work or in some other social context during the week, ☞ **giving them a quick phone call is usually the best way to do this**. It sets the issue of your support just enough apart from your normal, everyday communication to help the potential supporter realise that this is about something a bit different and a bit special. Although you'll feel a bit nervous doing it, ☞ **make sure that you mention the reason for your call near the start of the conversation**, otherwise the other person will be wondering why you've called! Even if you think that they already know, ☞ **outline in brief your need for support and explain that you'd like to meet with them to see if they would like to be part of your support team**. The phone is a good medium for making appointments, but it's not the best way to hold a detailed conversation about a topic as important as your support.

If an opportunity crops up in some other context for you to set up a time to meet, then by all means use it. If over coffee after church someone asks you how your plans are going, then it would be a bit daft to say that you will call them later to set up an appointment to tell them! Again these casual coffee-after-church-type chats are best used to set up a time to talk in more depth about your plans and your support. Don't dump it all on someone when they really weren't expecting it.

> *The purpose of the call is to arrange to meet, not to raise support, so don't get dragged into long explanations over the phone.*

However you do it, you will develop a style that suits you, but by the end of your phone call (or casual chat) there are some key elements that the person you are asking for an appointment needs to know:

- that you are contacting them for a special reason
- the stage you are at in your entry into (or continuation of) whatever aspect of Christian ministry you are involved in
- that your work in Christian ministry is dependent on you building up a financial support team
- that you particularly want to talk to them about being part of your financial support team
- that it is clear when and where you will meet.

Rob called us to ask if we were free to come for supper that Saturday. As it happened, we were free and were delighted to accept. Rob and Kay had been on the fringe of our circle of acquaintances for a couple of years and we didn't really know them that well, so we were looking forward to finding out a bit more about them.

Although we hadn't visited Rob and Kay before, they struck me as an informal, 'cracked mug in the kitchen' type couple. But when we arrived, the best linen tablecloth was out, as was the best china. I'm normally the cynic, but it was Phyllis who leant over and whispered, "There's more to this than just supper".

It was a great meal and totally enjoyable, until the coffee arrived. It was then that Rob sprung his surprise, asking us if we could do him and Kay a significant favour. It all became painfully clear. There had been a hidden agenda lurking under the table all evening, just waiting for the right moment to pounce.

Suddenly I felt a bout of indigestion coming on, despite the delights of the meal we'd just enjoyed. When Rob had called to invite us for supper, he hadn't been able to bring himself to be up-front about the main reason for the invitation. To counter his feeling of awkwardness about asking someone they didn't know well for help, he and Kay had gone overboard to make us feel special. But when he suddenly sprang his request on me, it felt more as if Phyllis and I had been 'buttered up'. I ended up feeling cheated, bribed and trapped.

I'm sure that Rob was totally oblivious to the feelings all this created in me as I listened uncomfortably to his request. I explained that I wasn't the best person to offer the help he needed. It was true, but I must admit that my response was driven at least as much by the feelings of being set up as it was by the reality of my inadequacy in fulfilling his particular needs.

If Rob had just explained why he was calling and asked if we could have a chat about it over a cup of coffee, I'd have been happy to meet him and discuss the issue. I think that I'd still have suggested that he find someone more qualified to fulfil his request, but it would have been much easier all round if we'd both known the real reason for his phone call.

Because Rob wasn't prepared to take the discomfort of a more open approach, I ended up being the one feeling uncomfortable.

☞ Rob wasn't asking for support, but the principle still applies. Don't ask for support without first of all asking for permission to ask for support. Hidden agendas are the scourge of the British Christian church – don't add to them!

Here's what it might sound like:

I have invented two scenarios that will crop up as examples throughout the rest of the book. One sees Claire Lewis, a 28-year-old single woman raising support to go to Turkey to work with Mid Med mission. The other involves Jim Martin, married to Sue, in their mid to late 40s and with two children. Jim is going to work with Declare, a UK-based evangelism organisation. He'll be working in their office in Stoke as their IT manager and general admin person. Jim and Sue first came across Declare when they ran an evangelism course in their church. Sue is a nurse and will keep her part-time nursing job at a local hospital to help the family finances, but she would love to be more involved with Declare herself.

Both examples are fictional and I realise that their situations, responses and actions will not be the same as yours. But there should be something in one, or even both, that you can build on for your support-raising.

Let's look at Claire first:

She has just been accepted to work with Mid Med Mission, a Christian organisation that brings practical and spiritual help to the peoples of North Africa and the Middle East. Mid Med has been in existence, in various forms, since the 1890s. Claire is currently an English teacher in Sheffield and will be working in an English Language Centre in a Kurdish city in eastern Turkey. The centre was set up about ten years ago by Mid Med Mission and Claire's main task will be leading English language classes. She will also be involved helping a small local church that grew out of a summer team a few years ago from Operation Outreach, an evangelism group that works closely with Mid Med.

Claire is contacting Jenny, a PE teacher in the same school in Sheffield. They used to go to the same church until Claire moved to a church plant in a new housing estate in another part of the city two years ago. Neither of them is from Sheffield originally. They started teaching at the school on the same day five years ago. It was the first teaching job for them both and they quickly became good friends. They shared a house together with a couple of other teachers for three years, but then Jenny bought a small one-bedroomed flat on a 95 per cent mortgage to try to get her foot on the property ladder.

Claire is from a Christian family in Newcastle and became a Christian as a child. Jenny isn't and became a Christian during her last year at Southampton University. Her family lives in Bromsgrove.

Their school has a split campus and they tend to be in the two different parts of the school so they don't bump into each other that much at work.

It is a Monday evening in late May and Claire has phoned Jenny.

Jenny, this is Claire. How's things?

> *Great. Still recovering from the youth weekend. Those kids don't even know how to spell sleep!*

Yeh, I heard it went well. I hear that Peter Thompson made a commitment during the weekend? That's great news, what with all he's been through since his parents split up.

> *Yes, it was great. I think that five or six made commitments. The Saturday night was really special.*

You and the rest of the team put in a huge amount into those young people. Seeing God work in a special way like that must be a great encouragement.

Jenny, the main reason I called is to see if we can get together for an hour or so this week. As you know I've been accepted to work with Mid Med Mission and it looks like I'll be heading off to Turkey at the start of next year.

Yes, I'd heard that it had all worked out. It must be very exciting. How do you feel now that it's all actually happening? It seems ages since you first started talking about it.

It is ages! It took me a long time to get round to filling in the application form and then it's taken months to get through the whole application process. Then there was the TEFL course last summer and all that. Getting into teaching is easy compared to getting into mission work!

So it is going to be Turkey, then? At one stage wasn't there some talk of you going to Cyprus?

Yes, that's where the Mid Med main office is and I probably will be going there later next year for a couple of months' training, but it definitely looks like Turkey that I'll be working in. In the end it will depend on where the greatest need is at the time I'm going. Because I'm single I'm more likely to be asked to get involved in projects where it might be more difficult for a family with school-aged kids. I'm happy with that – anything for an adventure!

But about getting together. I'm not sure if you know, but the way Mid Med Mission works is that each of their staff develops around them a team of people who will support them with regular financial support, prayer and encouragement. There's no fixed salary or anything like that. It's just gifts from interested friends that cover my costs. I'm right at the start of building my support team and because we've been friends for so long, I'd really like you to be one of my first supporters. Could we meet up tomorrow after school for an hour or so?

You mean they don't pay you to do this? That sounds a bit risky? Is there a pension or anything?

Well, it is different. I've had to think through a lot of things in this, like the values I want to live by and that sort of thing. But we can chat more about it when we meet up. Would tomorrow be OK for you?

Yes, I think so. No, wait, I might have a department meeting right after school tomorrow. Not sure. Can't even check it – I've left my diary in school. Just to be safe, can we make it Wednesday?

Wednesday would do fine. Can you come round to my classroom at the end of classes and we can head out to that new coffee shop near St Mary's, the one you were raving about last week?

Sounds good. Tell me more about how this whole support thing works anyhow. It all sounds a bit scary to me, especially when you're used to just getting a salary at the end of each month!

I'm just getting used to the thought of it myself, to tell you the truth, but I'll explain all about in on Wednesday.

OK, I'll look forward to it. Not sure how much I can help, but I'd like to do something.

So, we'll meet in my classroom after school on Wednesday.

Given my head for detail, you'd better remind me on Wednesday.

Sure. I'll text you sometime in the morning.

While there may be patterns that you will begin to recognise as you start talking to people about your support, there are also differences in each situation. Begin thinking about what in your relationship would make it likely that that person would support you and what might be a difficulty.

Just from listening in to Jenny and Claire's conversation, you should be able to spot a few issues that Claire may need to keep in mind, especially as they relate to what we know about Jenny's values, personality and knowledge of mission support. I've given you a couple to start off with, along with an answer to one of them. See if you can find another two or three.

ISSUE: Jenny is scatty and forgets details

IMPLICATION: Claire will need to keep the initiative to help Jenny complete whatever support commitment she might make.

ISSUE: Jenny asked twice about the financial security of Claire's decision. Jenny has also taken out a 95 per cent mortgage to get her foot on the property ladder.

IMPLICATION:

ISSUE:

IMPLICATION:

ISSUE:

IMPLICATION:

ISSUE:

IMPLICATION:

CHAPTER 16

THE COFFEE-CUP CONVERSATION

Meet up

Having set up a time to meet someone to talk about your support, then the next step is to meet them, ideally over a cup of coffee or a meal. By this stage you will need to have a good idea of:

- **what you want to say**
- **perhaps some visual way of explaining it** (we'll look at this in more detail later – see Support Presentation Album on pages 200–204)
- **some promotional material about your mission or project**
- **whatever a person needs to get their support to you** – standing order form, Gift Aid declaration, etc.

Let's look at how to prepare what to say in more detail

As you think about sitting down with a friend, explaining what God is calling you into and asking them if they would like to be part of your support team, my guess is that you might be feeling a bit uneasy. How will it go? What will they think? What if they say no? What if they say yes!?

In the previous section we looked at what can make the asker feel uncomfortable. But we also looked at what can make the potential supporter feel uncomfortable. Remember, discomfort doesn't go away, it simply transfers to the other person. This might be a good

Look back at pages 95–121

time to review this section and to begin getting used to taking the discomfort yourself, so that the supporter can be at ease in the process as much as possible.

What your work will be about

Most of those who will support you will do so primarily because of their exisiting relationship with you, not because of an interest in the organisation you are joining or the specific work you'll be doing. Any interest they do have is likely to be as the result of your enthusiasm.

Their starting point in understanding what you'll be doing is much further back than yours, so don't overwhelm them with detail they can't relate to. The best way to explain any issue or cause is to **tell people-stories**. This is what Jesus tended to do when explaining the Kingdom of God, surely one of the most complex of subjects: simple people-stories that explain a great truth and in their simplicity and immediacy even young children understand them.

Remember also that the reason you are planning to do this work is because there are people who need to hear and see God's love for them. No matter what area of Christian service you are getting involved in, and no matter if you will be at the cutting edge of some dynamic new and innovative evangelism ministry or working behind a desk in a mission office, **keep in the forefront of your mind the person who will ultimately benefit from your work**. Placing your work in the context of a need in people's lives that is being met, rather than just the activity of the work itself, will make it easier for people to relate to what you'll be doing.

Keeping the conversation focused

Although each person you contact – or who contacts you – about support will have a different starting point in the discussion, there is a general flow of information that will help them make an informed decision about supporting you. Putting it in a workbook like this can make it seem very linear – step one, step two, step three, etc until you reach the all important ask. Conversations don't flow like that. They tend to weave in and out of the main theme, with a few tangents, helpful or otherwise, thrown in on the way to some sort of conclusion.

In this case you do have a destination for the conversation. You want the person to be able to decide whether or not they want to be part of your support team, so it will need to be a conversation with some sort of structure rather than just a vague verbal ramble.

See pages 110–111

But it can't be a monologue, with the potential supporter feeling that they are being 'processed' through your well-crafted presentation. Remember the story of the role-play by the couple going to Indonesia? ☞ **Re-read it** and beware the 'fixed script' approach. Yes, you need to be prepared. Yes, you need to have some structure to the conversation. Yes, you need to have a destination in mind for the discussion. But you may need to let the conversation weave its way around a bit to get there.

What information is the potential supporter looking for?

If I were choosing whether or not I'd support you, this is the sort of information I'd need to know:

- What **needs** are you, or your organisation, addressing?
- How has your organisation been **addressing these needs** over the years?
- How is your organisation addressing these needs in the **specific area of work** you'll be involved in?
- What will **you** be doing and what has led you into this?
- What sort of **support** are you looking for from me, that will make it possible for you to do what you're planning to do?
- Is this the sort of **commitment** I'd like to make?

Depending on the potential supporter's existing relationship with you, they will already know the answers to these questions to a greater or lesser extent. But don't assume too much. All the time that you've been immersed in the application process, learning about the organisation, thinking about this major change in your life, they have been busy with their own life, job, family, etc. They may not be as up to speed with your life as you think. **Using phrases like "you might already know" allows you to impart information, even if the person does already know it.**

Now we'll look at what this might end up sounding like in Claire's case when she meets up with Jenny. In Chapter 17 we'll look at the planning stage from Jim's perspective. Then in Chapter 18 it will be over to you, and a chance to think through and write down some of the answers you can give your own potential supporters to the questions I've listed above. So you will end up with a basic plan for what you're likely to say when you talk to people about your support.

167

Here's what it might sound like (abridged version)

Read through the way the meeting goes between Claire and Jenny. Notice how Claire manages to keep the conversation focused so that she covers all the points listed on the previous page.

It's Wednesday afternoon. Claire and Jenny are sitting over a cup of coffee, as arranged. Jenny has had a bad day in school, with a particularly difficult class in the afternoon. They bemoan the discipline of the pupils in the school in general (a common topic of conversation in the staff room) and the behaviour of Year 9 in particular (an even more common topic of conversation!).

Claire uses this as a chance to bring up the impending big changes in her life:

Well, come the end of first term next year, I'll be gone!

> *Lucky you! Mind you, I'm not sure if I'd go as far as you're going just to escape the scourge of Year 9! So how does it feel now that it's all official?*

A bit of mixed feelings I suppose. It's what I've wanted to do since I was a child, be a missionary. I remember when I went for an interview with the head of my secondary school when I was moving up from primary school, he asked me what I wanted to do when I left school. I said, "Be a missionary". He looked at my dad and said, "Passing fancy, I suppose." My dad said, "Don't think so!" At least it was a bit different from all the other career choices he heard that day!

> *So this has been working on you for a long time, then?*

Yes, I can't really remember a time when I didn't want to be some sort of missionary. I blame it all on the missionary biographies I got as Sunday School prizes!

> *It's strange. When I was a kid I had no idea that missionaries still existed. I suppose I thought they went out with Queen Victoria and the Empire.*

Missionaries are a much hardier breed than that. It would take a lot more than the collapse of an empire to wipe them out!

So what exactly will you be doing in Turkey?

Well, I'll be living away at the eastern side of the country, in a city not that far from the Iraqi border actually. Mid Med Mission has had a team working with the Kurdish people in that region for a few years, mostly involved in community health and education projects. I'll be working in an English centre set up about ten years ago by Operation Outreach, which is a Christian organisation that Mid Med works with in the area. My main work will be teaching English, but I guess that the students will be a lot more eager to learn than Year 9 were today. There's also a small church in the area that grew out of an Operation Outreach summer project about five years ago.

I bet it'll be a lot different from St Philip's too!

I'm sure it will! There's a Turkish couple who now head up the work in the church and I understand that Mid Med staff from the West tend to keep a low profile in the church, mostly just working on an individual basis.

So how long has this Med Mid group been going?

It's Mid Med. It's been going for about 110 years in different forms.

[Here follows a lengthy and winding discussion about Claire's proposed work, the history of Mid Med Mission, the rights of the Kurdish people, the political instability of the whole region, the importance of literacy, changing trends in mission, the needs of an emerging national church and other assorted and semi-related topics! It is all liberally laced with people-stories from the region that Claire had gleaned from other Mid Med people she's met and also from her own trip to Turkey a couple of summers ago. Jenny doesn't bring up the subject of support, so it's up to Claire to broach the subject.]

So, like I said the other day, the first step in this for me, once I got accepted, is to begin building a financial support team.

Yeh, what's that all about? Doesn't the mission or the church or somebody just pay you?

Well, it doesn't work like that. I know that the church will give something, but there's no way they could cover anything like all my costs. And the mission itself has no big pot of central funds that they can pay people out of.

In fact, by getting each staff member to raise their support from their own friends it means that the mission doesn't have to have a massive impersonal fundraising campaign to raise all the funds it would need to pay everybody. And, from my side of things, it means that I'm being supported by people I know, people who are likely to pray for me as well. If it was all paid from a central pot then there would be no real relationship between the givers and the missionaries, all a bit remote and anonymous.

But isn't it all a bit insecure? You'll have no guarantee of anything at the end of the month. Teaching mightn't pay a lot, but at least a secure salary comes with the job.

Well, I've thought about that and working with Mid Med is actually a lot more secure than teaching.

How's that?

Well, right now I have only one source of income – the teaching job. Remember a couple of years ago when we had four teachers made redundant because of falling numbers in the school? Thankfully, we were in just ahead of the four who lost their jobs, but it was close. At least with Mid Med I'll have 20 to 30 sources of income, a whole range of people who will be supporting me on a regular basis. If, for whatever reason, one has to drop out, it wouldn't be the end of the job; it'd just mean that I'd need to add on another supporter. And anyway, it's God who is calling me into this. He has enough wealth at his disposal to take care of me!

I'd never thought of it like that. Still seems a bit risky to me. And don't you find it all a bit embarrassing, asking people for money and all. I know that I couldn't do it.

I must admit I was a bit intimidated at the start, when I first heard how it all worked. I'm still a bit nervous about it, but I know that this is where God wants me to be, so it'll work out. And if you're not embarrassed talking about it, I'm not either!

So how much do you need to find? Is it OK to ask?

Sure, no problem. It works out at just over £10,000 per year, about £850 per month. That includes an amount for normal living costs, some for day-to-day ministry expenses, some for back-office costs that are needed to help get me to Turkey and keep me there, a bit for health insurance and even a bit goes to a pension fund. It'd be a lot more if I was married and had kids.

Just as well you stayed single then! Sounds like this mission has it all organised. But it sounds like you're not going to get rich working with them. What's their name again?

Mid Med Mission – you're going to have to do better than that remembering it! And I suppose if I wanted to get rich I'd choose something else – probably not teaching either, mind you.

That's for sure! So how does this support work in practice. What would I need to do?

Well, I'm looking for key people like you who will give, pray and be an encouragement. As far as the giving goes, most of my expenses will be regular, so giving monthly by standing order would be best. As for the praying and encouraging, from what I hear there are a few internet cafés in the area, so even if I can't get online all the time, at least I'll be able to keep in touch from time to time to keep you up to date with things.

Sounds like you've got it organised too! Yeh, I'd love to help. I really admire what you're doing, giving up your career to do this. But I suppose it seems just the right fit for you. I'm not sure how much I can help, though. The mortgage is still taking too much each month. Is there a set amount people give or what?

No, it's entirely up to you. If it helps, I'm looking for a few people at the start who could give somewhere between £75–£100 per month, a few others who could give £50–£75 per month and a few others between £25 and £50. Of course, it can be below or above these amounts, but these are the sorts of amounts that would really help get the support going.

Well, I know that it won't be at the top end, but I could maybe do around £30 at this stage. I'd need to take a look at how things stand before I settle on an amount. Would that be OK?

That'd be great. My decision to work with Mid Med has been a serious one for me and I'd like to make sure that those on the support team take it seriously as well. Let me leave the standing order form with you and also the Gift Aid declaration – you know how Gift Aid works ?

Yeh, I just sign it and you get the tax back, or something like that. I've signed one for the church.

That's right. It adds another 28 per cent to your giving – so it would make your £30 equal to almost £40. Money for nothing and too good to throw away. Could I check back with you in a couple of days? Would that be enough time for you to decide?

A couple of days should be fine. I'll let you know before the end of the week.

Great. Just in case we don't bump into each other during the week or you forget or anything, is it OK if I give you a call at the weekend?

I'm going down to Bromsgrove to see my folks this weekend, but you can always grab me in the staff room some day next week.

OK, so long as one of us gets the other one at some stage!

Look, thanks for asking me about this. I haven't really got my giving sorted out yet and I've been meaning to do something about it. I give a bit to the church, but I know that I should be doing more. I know that the finances have been tight for the past couple of years, but I've felt a bit bad that I haven't got my giving a bit more organised, so this is important for me too.

[The conversation then reverts back to Year 9 and how many of them are likely to end up enjoying a stay at Her Majesty's pleasure at some stage in their lives!]

This fictional conversation is between two women in their late-20s who know each other well. If Claire had been talking to her former Sunday School teacher from her home church in Newcastle, the style and content would have been a bit different.

Claire even included a few comments that challenged Jenny's strong focus on depending on visible financial security, and this prompted a response from Jenny that she really did need to get her giving sorted out. In some cases, your request for support will bring a person forward in their understanding and practice of giving, a lot more than the limited teaching they are likely to have heard in their church.

After meeting with Jenny, Claire will still have two specific stages remaining in the process I outlined on page 157:

- saying thank you
- and following up her conversation.

Saying thank you

> A note to the guys. Card manufacturers seem to think that it is only women who send thank you cards, so they tend to be a bit too pink and flowery for the average macho-man. If you find a thank you card that you like, or even a good blank card, buy lots of them!

No matter what response you get from the person you have spoken to about your support, ☞ **write a thank you note within a day**, even if it is someone you see regularly. The note reinforces that you are interested in them joining your support team (as opposed to just anybody), allows you to reinforce a couple of the key points from your conversation and, where appropriate, can act as a reminder that you will contact them to find out their decision. Even if they have said that they can't support you at this time, you need to send a thank you note, expressing your appreciation for them thinking about it and asking for their prayers for something specific that is coming up in your plans.

Follow-up

In most cases you will need to contact the potential supporter again for some reason before the process is completed. Depending on how far on they were in their ability to decide when you were speaking to them and what next steps were agreed when you met, this could be to find out their decision, find out how much they have decided to support you by, pick up the standing order form or answer some question they raised during your discussion.

If you have been keeping good records as you've gone along, you will have noted somewhere in your system when you are to contact them again and what this is for.

There are various points in this whole process when you'll be tempted to back off, not to pursue a discussion any further. And this is often one of those points.

Remember you may have to keep the initiative. Make sure you do all the things you've said you will do. And if days go by and they don't ring you back and you start to worry that they aren't as interested in your support as you first thought, look back again at the example in Chapter 7. ☞ **Do them a favour. Pick up the phone and call them.** Will you feel a bit uncomfortable? Of course you will. You'll probably need to apologise for not getting back to them sooner. But whatever discomfort you feel will be a lot less than the mixture of negative feelings they'll feel when they get your first prayer letter from wherever it is you're going and realise that they never quite got round to supporting you. By now, they surmise, it's probably too late. And seeing you've actually gone, you probably don't need their support.

You've missed out on a supporter. They've missed out on being part of whatever it is God has called you to.

> If you think you've left it too late with someone like this, put this book down and go and phone them now. It'll only feel even more uncomfortable tomorrow.

CHAPTER 17

"But It's Not as Simple as That for Me…"

At this stage I can just hear Jim. *"It's alright for Claire. She's single, with a reasonably low support target. And she's going somewhere exotic. She has been a Christian for years, her family are probably supportive of what she's doing and she must have lots of Christian friends all over the place. I'm in my late 40s, with a wife and two children. Sue and I became Christians just eight years ago and we're the only Christians in our two families. We know almost no Christians outside our own church. On top of this, I'm just going to Stoke – great place, but not really as exotic as eastern Turkey! And all I'll be doing will be working in Declare's office, looking after their computer system. I was made redundant a couple of years ago and all the redundancy money has gone on keeping us alive since then as well as putting me through Bible College. Declare want me to raise as much of my £20,000 salary as I can. I've no hope of coming anywhere close to this!"*

OK, so what should Jim do?

He should do just the same as Claire.

He should identify people he thinks might be interested; ask if he can talk to them about the exciting changes in his life and how they could be part of it; then sit down with them and share his heart.

Jim might still come back with the argument that it really won't work, because of all the negatives he's listed above and that no one will be interested in supporting him.

But how does he know? Has he asked them? Or is Jim guilty of answering for people even before he has asked them the question?

Yes, there are differences in the two situations. And, yes, they may well mean that people look at Jim's role differently from Claire's.

Let's take a look at some heart and head issues that Jim will need to get sorted before his hands will get fully working on raising his support.

First of all, we are **all** different, uniquely created by God with different personalities, different gifting, different family backgrounds and different calls of God on our lives. **All God ever asks us to do is to faithfully respond to whatever he asks of us.** He never promises us that it will be easy (just read the second half of Hebrews 11 to see what happened to some people who lived a life of faithful response to God!) but he does promise that if we are faithful to him, he will be faithful to us – although not always in the ways we expect.

Yes, it is true that raising support for what can be perceived to be a low-emotion job in a low-emotion location in a low-emotion organisation involved in low-emotion activity can be a challenge. It shouldn't be, but it is. **Is Jim's decision to use his gifts and abilities to help advance God's Kingdom any less a call of God than Claire's?** No, it isn't. But too many people think that it is. They might not say so outright, but by being more willing to fund people in the supposedly more glamorous aspects of ministry, their gifts demonstrate what their minds think.

Thomas Walter Wilson

Have you ever heard of Thomas Walter Wilson? Probably not.

Ever heard of Billy Graham? Unless you've lived the life of a complete hermit since the mid-1940s, you most certainly will have. T W Wilson (known as just 'T' to his friends) was a boyhood friend of Billy Graham who became his right-hand man during his heyday. It was 'T' who made sure the plans were all in place, who anticipated the problems and got them solved before they happened, the man Billy Graham relied on for advice and who looked after all the details that were necessary for the big campaigns to run smoothly.

Do you remember seeing T W Wilson up there preaching? No, he was beavering away behind the scenes so that Billy Graham was up there preaching. Which of them was the more important during their days working together? They were equally important, not because of the jobs they did, but because they were both faithfully following God's call on their lives. One happy in the forefront of public ministry; the other happy working away in the background.

So how do we deal with the support challenges of those who work in the background, freeing up the more public people to do their work?

In many cases, organisations deal with this challenge by simply removing it and paying their home-based staff, and especially their office-based staff, a salary from centrally-raised funds.

While I understand the expediency of this choice, there are inherent dangers in it. First of all, it perpetuates the idea that people like Jim aren't real missionaries. It is also a bit of a misnomer to say that people are paid from 'central funds'. The money that is used to pay them also comes from supporters, but they are usually supporters who the individual staff member doesn't know, people who don't really pray specifically for the individual staff members and whose gift could well be used for other aspects of ministry. More importantly, it can leave Jim and those like him spiritually unprotected.

> *Interserve, a well-known mission with a focus in Asia, asked if I'd give a support-training seminar for their UK-based promotion, personnel and admin staff. As one of their leaders put it, "We ask our missionaries going overseas to raise the money and prayer they need for their work. But we don't do it ourselves. Not only is this a case of 'don't do as I do, do as I say', but we realise that, because we don't have that strong personal link with a team of supporters, we are not as keenly prayed for as our overseas staff are. Our work in the UK is critical in ensuring that those at the coal-face of mission are able to work at their fullest potential. Yet we are in danger of being the weakest link spiritually. We daren't let this happen. We need to have a support team around us too." A wise choice from a mature group.*

Jim needs to recognise that **the call God has put on his life is as worthy of receiving financial support from God's people as anyone else's**. He also needs to make sure that he doesn't confuse his job description with his cause. Yes, he'll be sitting all day making sure that network servers do their job, that the new database software is functioning as it should, that the staff who need training in various IT tasks get trained, and generally trying to perform IT miracles with a limited budget.

Jim isn't joining Declare just because he likes sitting in front of a computer screen all day. He could get a lot more money, with a lot less hassle, doing the same type of work in the sort of IT job he'd been in for years. He has made the choice to work with Declare **because it is his way of using the gifts and expertise that God has built into his life to help other people hear about God's love**.

"But it's not as simple as that for me…"

Declare equips churches to be more effective in their evangelism. They run evangelism training courses, mentor young evangelists, produce contemporary evangelism material, organise joint-church evangelism initiatives and generally try to help Christians to be more confident and relevant in sharing their faith. Unlike Mid Med Mission, Declare is a young organisation, started just nine years ago by an evangelist who was keen to see others share their faith. They have aspirations to have a national impact, even international, but at this stage most of their work is within 40 miles of Stoke. They don't have a high profile and few outside those immediately involved in the mission would even know they exist.

All this means that Jim and Sue don't even have the luxury of a well-known mission to help them with their support-raising. At the outset, they will need to focus their attentions on those who know them well: those who recognise the courageous steps they have taken and the way they have been faithful to God's leading as fairly new Christians themselves.

Rather than becoming daunted by the seemingly impossible task of finding £20,000, they should **break the process down into bite-sized tasks.** Start by asking, *"If God only allowed us to have one supporter, who would we like to have on our team?"* They're not likely to choose the wealthiest person they know. They are more likely to choose someone who has been an encouragement to them, someone who has built into their lives.

After approaching that person, they should then ask themselves, *"If God allowed us another two supporters, who would they be?"* And, after talking to these potential supporters, they should keep going, one and two at a time.

Because Jim's day-to-day work lacks the 'glamour' of Claire's job, he will need to talk as much as he can about the evangelism aspects of Declare's work, with a liberal scattering of people-stories about people who have become Christians as a result of their work. He will also need to tell stories of people and churches whose confidence in sharing their faith have been enhanced through Declare. **Although Jim won't be involved directly in evangelism training as his daily work, without Jim and the others who keep Declare operating effectively, these stories wouldn't be there to be told.**

SUMMARY

If Jim and Sue focus on all the reasons that make their support difficult, they could well end up being overwhelmed by the task. But by focusing on a few key principles, they can turn a heavy burden into a light burden, worked out with a passion.

- Recognise that **God** is your provider, not the organisation you'll work with, your support system or even your supporters.

- Recognise that following God's call isn't just a nice idea, it is being faithful to God's call on your life.

- Break down your support target to manageable intermediate targets.

- Work at your support one person at a time, starting with close friends who will support you even if you make a mess of your presentation to them!

- Expect God to do the abnormal as well as the normal in your support.

- Be ready to respond to the abnormal opportunities as soon as they appear.

- Don't despair if it doesn't all happen as quickly as you would like; God's timing doesn't always walk hand in hand with ours.

"But it's not as simple as that for me…"

Notes

CHAPTER 18

JOIN THE SCOUTS

See key points outlined on page 167

I like the Scouts' motto: Be Prepared. It certainly beats the opposite: Be Unprepared! Whether or not you were ever a Scout or a Guide, it's time to join up, at least to the Be Prepared bit.

No matter what the set of relationships or the personalities, there are common threads that should weave their way through any support conversation.

You will want to keep the flow natural and informal. It should be a chat between friends, or at least two people with some personal connection, not a cold-call, double-glazing sales pitch. Even if it's somebody you don't know that well or maybe somebody you haven't seen for a while, for some reason you have thought that they might be interested in supporting you and they have agreed to talk about it. This should give you enough confidence to relax a bit during your conversation with the potential supporter. **You might still have butterflies in your stomach about it, but at least they should be flying in formation!**

Although it may seem a bit false and contrived at the outset, being prepared and having a good idea of what you plan to say will ensure that you are more relaxed when talking to people about your support. It will also help you keep the conversation on track and, if necessary, bring it back on track if it goes too far down a totally irrelevant tangent.

By contrast, if you go into a support appointment without having thought through what you want to say and without some sort of structure in mind for the conversation, you are much more likely to forget key bits of information, be unclear at important points in the discussion and leave the person you are talking to unsure about what you are asking them to do.

Your support presentation outline

Jot down words or short phrases for each section. Remember, this is to give you the basis for what you'll say to people. The points follow the outline on page 167. What you will actually say will change from person to person, depending on who the person is and how well you know them.

As an example, I've included the sort of things that Jim and Sue might have jotted down. This page assumes that you are working with an organisation. If you are working independently, then simply answer the questions for yourself.

1. What **needs** are you or your organisation addressing?
   - unchurched society
   - lack of confidence in evangelism
   - few role models for young evangelists
   - little culturally relevant evangelism

2. In general terms, **how has your organisation been addressing these needs** over the years?
   - evangelism training
   - mentored young evangelists
   - creative local evangelism initiatives
   - church-based evangelism internships

3. How is your organisation addressing these needs **in the specific area of work you'll be involved in**?
   - major expansion
   - need to get firm admin base
   - free up leadership to focus on evangelism
   - improved communication with integrated IT system

4. **What will you be doing** and what has led you into this?
   - own unchurched background
   - misconceptions about God and Jesus
   - encouraged by Declare's approach
   - redundancy
   - desire to use skills to further effective evangelism
   - want to see other unchurched people come to Christ
   - oversee admin and IT
   - Sue part-time mentoring young women evangelists

5. **What sort of support are you looking for from people?**
   - can't do this alone
   - no large pot of central funds
   - need team to be part of this
   - regular
   - money – only source of income
   - prayer – spiritual battle
   - encouragement – major adjustments

6. Is this the sort of **commitment this particular potential supporter would like to make**?
   - need key people
   - people at different support levels
   - support in by March
   - identify why we're asking this person
   - would you like to join the team?

Making it Work

Your support presentation outline

☞ Take some time to think through what a potential supporter needs to know in order to make an informed decision about your support.

☞ Use the page opposite or a blank page to jot down some basic headings and main points, but don't write it as a script.

☞ Practise speaking it out loud, using your notes as a prompt.

☞ Then write down more fully what you have said. We tend to speak much more informally than we write, so writing down what you speak will be a lot more help than speaking what you write down.

Use this space to begin writing your support presentation.

Join the Scouts

Create your own role-play!

Once you've got some basic idea of what you need to include in your conversation to help the person make an informed decision about supporting you, flesh it out a bit, especially with people-stories that will illustrate the points you want to make.

☞ **Early on, get a friend to practise on.** You could even make it a real role-play and actually ask a good friend for support, while also asking them for honest feedback on what you say. They'll know you well enough not only to be delighted to help, but also to give you support even if you get it totally wrong! If they say things like, "No idea what you meant, but I think you want me to give you money" or "Sounds great – just wish I had got a chance to say something", then you've a bit more work to do before unleashing yourself on the unsuspecting public of your extended network of contacts. But at least having a friend who has heard how you communicated to them will mean that you will have someone who is likely to pray even more for you as you approach others!

☞ **If you can't get a willing conscript, then practise saying it out loud**, at least pretending to be speaking to a real person. Then think:

- if you were the person you had been talking to, would they have understood enough of what you were saying and what you were asking them to do to be able to make an intelligent and informed decision about supporting you?
- would they relate to it from their perspective?

You might well feel like an idiot, standing in front of a mirror talking to yourself. But better to look an idiot in front of a mirror than in front of a potential supporter. The purpose of this is not so that you can get a slick presentation down pat. Rather it is to ensure that you make sense when talking to real people in real situations.

It is said of sermons that either the preacher sweats in the preparation or the congregation sweats during the presentation! With support-raising, if you don't sweat preparing what you'll say, then you and the potential supporter are both likely to sweat as you mumble and wobble your way through some incomprehensible monologue!

> Far from restricting you, being prepared allows you to speak freely from the heart, confident that you are covering all the main points that need to be discussed.

A word of warning

What you say needs to come from the heart, not from a script. Take enough time over this to ensure that your preparation helps you be relaxed and leaves you in more control of the discussion. If you short-circuit this stage you could end up being controlled by your preparation, rather than vice versa.

Make the supporter's life easier

You will also need to have with you whatever the potential supporter needs to send in their support. Some missions use personal profile brochures for their new staff, with a smiling photo on the front page, opening out to some background about the new staff member, details of where they will be working and some general information about the organisation, including how the staff are supported. These work, but only up to a point.

In most cases there is a tear-off panel at the end with a range of tick boxes:

- ❏ I'd like the prayer letter
- ❏ I'd be interested in supporting regularly
- ❏ enclosed is a special gift
- ❏ please add me to the organisation's mailing list…

that sort of thing. This is then sent back to the mission office – once the person has dug the leaflet out of wherever it has been since they carried it home from the meeting, has ticked all the relevant boxes, filled in their details, found an envelope in a drawer somewhere and checked the form for the right address to send it to and posted it.

These are fine for giving out at meetings, or giving to friends as a bit of background. If you've ever gone coarse fishing, it's a bit like scattering some bait around the area you plan to fish in – it won't catch anything, but it should attract some fish to come and investigate. **But if you think that a profile leaflet like this will do your support-raising for you, you'll be badly disappointed.** If you assume that no one will ever send in the reply panel, you might be pleasantly surprised. As a matter of interest, when was the last time you filled in and posted a reply coupon like this, where there was no preaddressed envelope provided? If you are like me, at best it is something you will do tomorrow. At worst, it is just too much bother.

☞ **Always, always, always keep standing order forms with you. You never know when you might need one.**

Step 1.   Step 2

Where possible, ☞ **pick up the completed form yourself or have it posted back to you**, not to the mission office, in spite of what it might say on the form! If it is sent straight back to the office, when will you hear that the completed form has been returned?

A few of the groups I work with, but just a few, will email or phone a staff member within a day or two to let them know that a new standing order had been sent in for them. With some of the others it can be two months, or even longer, before the staff member finds out about new regular support. In the meantime, the staff member and supporter might have met a few times. Because the staff member isn't aware that the completed form has been sent in, they don't thank the supporter. But, as far as the supporter is concerned, the support has already been sent, so why doesn't the staff member mention it?

Better safe than sorry. ☞ **Make sure that the form comes to you so you can check that it has been completed correctly, note it in your records and thank the supporter.** Just make sure that you send it on to the office yourself as soon as you get it!

> I was leading a short evening support-training session for the new staff of Wycliffe Bible Translators. At the end one of the participants came up and said she'd like to support us. I'd never met her before and all I knew about her was that she was planning to go overseas as a missionary. I handed her the standing order form and Gift Aid declaration that I always keep tucked inside my Bible, assuming that she would want to talk a bit more about our work and perhaps take a day or so to think about the support. She asked if she could complete it then and there. I assured her that that would be fine with me. So she duly filled it in and handed it back, right there as we stood at the end of the seminar.

I had no intention of getting a new supporter that night. I hadn't even mentioned anything about us needing support. (We didn't. Our support was doing OK at that time.) But, for whatever reason, she wanted to support us. I headed off to my next meeting £20 per month better off than I'd been a couple of hours before. Be prepared.

> Alan had worked overseas for a number of years but, due to family reasons, had to return to the UK. He still kept in close contact with the mission and a few years later, when the family situation changed so that he could go overseas again, he re-joined the mission, starting his support-raising all over again. After contacting all those who had supported him previously, there was still some way to go to reach his support target, so he started contacting people who hadn't supported him the first time round, but who had shown interest in his work.
>
> Tim and Margaret were one such couple. They were delighted to support him but said that it was still likely to be the same level that they had given when Alan had been overseas before. Trying not to show his surprise at this news of previously unknown support, Alan thanked them, left them the necessary forms and went home.
>
> First thing the next morning, Alan phoned his mission's office and asked if the couple had ever sent in support for him. No, he was assured, but they had supported the mission's general ministry account at £30 per month for some years, but they had now stopped. Yes, coincidently, the years they had supported the general fund were the same years when Alan had been overseas.

Somewhere along the line, the system had broken down. Either Tim and Margaret hadn't specified on their support form that they wanted their support to go to Alan, or someone in the office had allocated it to the wrong account. Everyone concerned had been completely unaware of the mix up. Even in the most efficient offices, these things happen.

Tim and Margaret had assumed that they were supporting Alan all the years he was overseas. Alan, meanwhile, had no idea that they were as interested as they were in his work.

Alan was not a happy camper on hearing this news, but it convinced him of the importance of getting the completed support forms himself before they went to the office. That way, at least he could check if the support actually started to come to him in due course.

CHAPTER 19

POSTMAN PAT – CONTACTING PEOPLE BY LETTER

There are some people who it just isn't possible to see personally to explain about your plans to go into Christian ministry and to ask if they'd support you. In the case of the friend who now works in a bank in Singapore, it might be hard to justify the expense of going to see them to get £35 a month in support!

But think twice before dismissing the possibility of going to see someone who you really would like to be on your support team and who lives at the other end of the country. What would it mean to them if you took the time to go and see them? Most probably, it would seriously enhance their understanding that it wasn't just money from anybody you were chasing, but that you really did want to have them involved as part of your future plans. With low-cost airlines flying to more and more places, it may not cost as much as you think to see that friend in Exeter, Oban or wherever else might be the furthest point in the country from where you are.

But, sometimes it just doesn't work out.

Claire and Jenny – scenario 2

Let's take another look at the Claire/Jenny scenario and change some of the details around.

Jenny realised that she wasn't cut out for teaching. So two years ago she jumped at the chance of a job in an outward bound centre deep in the Scottish Highlands. The pay was a bit less, but a house came with the job, so Jenny sold her flat in Sheffield and bought a small house in Bromsgrove, near where her parents live. She lets out the house, with the rent just about covering her outgoings, but she sees it as a long-term investment.

Jenny has only been back to Sheffield twice, both times shortly after she left to sort out some complication about the sale of the flat. Claire promised a couple of times to go up to visit Jenny, but it hasn't worked out and now looks as though it won't. With Claire's family in Newcastle and Jenny's in Bromsgrove, there really isn't much chance that they'll get to meet up before Claire heads to Turkey.

Claire would still like Jenny to be one of her supporters. She doesn't feel comfortable about just phoning up to ask her; it would be dumping it all on Jenny without giving her the chance to think about it. Email could work (it's how they normally keep in touch, although even this is infrequent) but she knows that she'd need to write too much for an email. So she has settled on a letter.

Claire thinks that Jenny might have heard on the grapevine about her plans, but thinks that it's best to assume that she hasn't.

So what should a letter like this include?

- Acknowledge your existing relationship, your last contact, common interests, known struggles, etc.
- Bring the person up to date with what has happened to you recently.
- Explain about your organisation and what your particular role will be.
- Explain your need. The purpose of the letter is to give the person an opportunity to help – be specific.
- Ask for specific action based on the needs you have shared. Being specific helps the person understand what you expect from them.
- Acknowledge your relationship again, with an emphasis on thanks, appreciation, gratitude, partnership and commitment.
- Mention that you will call them in a few days to get their first thoughts on being part of your support team.
- Finish the letter and sign it.
- Often the first bit of a letter that people read is the PS, so add a note at the end to remind them that you would like them to respond by a certain date or that you will call them in a few days. On a busy morning when your letter arrives, it might just make the difference in it being read or not!
- It is useful to emphasise the important points in your letter, perhaps with <u>underlining</u>, CAPITALS, • bullet points or whatever style you prefer to use to make key words stand out.
- Enclose a response device, a stamped envelope addressed to you and a promotional leaflet from your organisation.

- The letter should be handwritten, if possible.
- Use personal writing paper and envelope rather than A4 paper and a business envelope; this is a letter from a friend and shouldn't look like the business post and junk mail that arrives with the same post.

Here's what it might look like:

Dear Jenny,

Hope this finds you well and enjoying life in the delights of the Highlands. How's the job working out? At least I presume those who come to your centre are there willingly and enthusiastically, which is more than could ever be said about Year 9's reluctant sorties to the gym in your time here.

The staff room hasn't been the same since you left — your sense of humour was always a good balance to the rampant cynicism of the rest of them.

Life here continues much as before. The new head seems to have made a bit of difference on the discipline front, but other than that there's not much change.

<u>Except that I'm leaving!</u>

Yes, you read it right. You might have already heard some of this on the bush telegraph, but come the end of first term next year I'm following your footsteps out of here, but not to the Scottish Highlands. I'm bound for even further afield and I'd like to see if you could help get me there. I'd love to sit down and talk this all through with you, but I doubt if I'll make it up to Inverness before I go and I don't expect that you've plans to visit Sheffield in the coming months, so a letter is the next best option.

As I'm sure you know, I've been interested in mission work for a long time and you might remember that I went to Turkey for a few weeks the summer you headed north. Well, I've followed up this interest and in the new year I head back to Turkey, this time for as long as God wants me there.

I'll be working with MID MED MISSION, an organisation that helps meet both the spiritual and physical needs of people in North Africa and the Middle East. I'm really excited about this new venture, and also a bit nervous.

I'll be working in an English Centre in a city in the Kurdish region of eastern Turkey, close, but not too close, to the Iraqi border. The centre was set up about 10 years ago by Operation Outreach, a Christian group that Mid Med works with quite closely. Mid Med has had a team working in this area for a few years, mostly involved in a range of public health and education projects. There is a small church nearby that grew out of an Operation Outreach summer team about five years ago. A Turkish couple now lead the church, but I understand that it has struggled to get accepted in the area, which is primarily Muslim. Mid Med staff from the West tend to keep a low profile in the church and work more on one-to-one relationships, which suits me just fine.

I'm really excited about the plans, especially working with the Kurds, who are the largest people group in the world without their own homeland, spread as they are across a number of countries, including Turkey and Iraq. They seem to have got a raw deal from everybody and, until recently, there was also little or no effective Christian witness to them as a group. Mid Med have made the Kurds a focal point for their prayers and work for the next few years. I've enclosed a brochure that gives more detail of Mid Med Mission.

So what did I mean when I said you could help me get there?

Well, the way Mid Med works is that, rather than have a huge impersonal fundraising campaign to raise the money to pay everybody from a central pot, each staff member builds up a group of friends who will support their work through regular financial support, regular prayers and regular encouragement.

I must admit that at the start I was a bit intimidated by the prospect of raising my own support. But the more I thought and prayed about it, the more I realised how important it was to go to Turkey with the commitment and backing of my friends, people who know me and people whose involvement I would really treasure.

The total I need to raise is just over £10,000 per year, or around £850 per month. This covers my normal living costs, day-to-day ministry expenses, Mid Med back-office costs and a bit for health insurance and pension fund. I've just started working on my support and so far I've been encouraged by the response of a few friends in the church and it looks like I've about £300 per month already pledged, including Gift Aid. The church will give something as well, but it will be next month (at least!) before they decide how much.

When I drew up a list of those I'd like to support me, your name was well up there! We went through so much together, especially in those early days in Sheffield, that I wouldn't want to launch into this next phase of my life without you being involved somehow.

Ideally what this would involve from you would be:

- giving some financial support – this will be the only source of income I'll have and because my expenses will tend to be regular, then the best option would be monthly support. (I've enclosed a standing order form that Mid Med staff use for this.)

- *praying for me and the people I'll be working with – I'm well aware that this will be a spiritual battlefield and I daren't go there unprotected.*
- *being an encouragement – it will be a lot different from Sheffield and I know that contact with friends like you will be important.*

From my side, I'll commit to keeping in touch as much as I can. Not sure if I'll be on-line where I'll be living, but I know that there are some internet cafés in the area, so at least we'll be able to keep in touch.

This whole venture is something that I simply can't do on my own and I'd be really delighted if you would be part of the team that make it happen.

In terms of the financial support, there's no fixed amount or anything. It's up to you, but if it helps, the average from individuals so far is around £40 per month with the top amount at £100. Feel free to come at, between, above or below these amounts! Of course, with Gift Aid whatever you give gets another 28% added – it's nice to get some tax back after these years of paying tax!

Would you think and pray about this for a couple of days? I'll give you a call towards the end of next week to get your thoughts on all this. I assume that your mobile number is still 07123 456 789? If not, I have the centre phone number and I'll get you through that. In the meantime if you've any questions about it, feel free to give me a call. My home number is the same (0114 234 5678) but my new mobile number is 07987 654 321. I've also enclosed a reply envelope for you to get the form back to me if you do sign up.

Thanks for thinking about this. Talk to you next week.

Yours,

Claire

P.S. I'll try to call on Thursday late afternoon. If that won't work, could you text me with a good time to call? Thanks.

So is that it?

No – the process isn't finished yet. No matter how good you think your letter is, no matter how well crafted the words or how friendly or personal it looks, **your letter is only useful if it gets read!** And if you are asking the person receiving the letter to respond in some way, it is only successful if the person not only realises that you are expecting them to respond but if they actually get round to doing something about it. There's too much that could go wrong just to leave your letter hanging there, hoping that it will all work.

Monday morning – your letter arrives...

...by Wednesday night – halfway down the pile

This sort of scenario happens. How do I know? Because I've a pile of papers littering the top of my desk. The ones that absolutely have to get replied to will get my attention: the car tax form, phone bill and so on. The others I'll get round to next week when things are easier. I suspect that I'm not alone in this approach to sorting priorities – a filing system for the critical and urgent, a piling system for everything else.

How do you get round this problem?...

... **By keeping the initiative yourself**, and not leaving it with the person who you're sending the letter to. As Claire did, add a line that says that you'll give them a call in a few days to get their thoughts on supporting you. It not only gives you the opportunity to phone them; it basically requires that you do.

If the person has read the letter, even if they had forgotten that you said you would call, they'll remember as soon as they hear your voice on the phone. There is always the chance that they are very organised and have taken time in advance of your call to think about their response, make their decision and be ready with their answer. But it is unlikely that your request for support will have dominated their agenda for sufficient time for them to have it all sorted out in that much detail. It is more likely that your call will stir them to action, often as far as them giving some response in principle over the phone, but without the detail worked out. It may well take a further call after another few days before it's all finalised.

If the person hasn't read the letter, it gives you the chance to say something like, *"No problem. The letter is to tell you some big news about my future and to see if you'd be able to help make it happen. It's just that I'd said in the letter that I'd give you a call to get your thoughts on it all. Could you have a look at it and I'll give you a call again in a couple of days? Would Wednesday night suit?"* You can be sure that they'll delve straight into the pile of post to find what it is that is so important that you've written to them and they'll be more ready the next time you call.

Be careful not to send too many letters at the same time, all saying that you'll call the person in a few days. Bear in mind that just getting hold of one person on the phone can often be a challenge!

Notes

CHAPTER 20

SHOW AND TELL

Responses from these close friends can give your support a good initial growth spurt. In many cases they may well even take the initiative to talk to you about support, some of them even offering support before you get accepted to do your work. It isn't unusual to get up to around 30 per cent of your support target quite quickly, and much of this can be raised without anything more than a good relationship to start with, a passion in your heart for what God's calling you to and a good clear discussion with your friends.

However, in most cases you will need to extend well beyond this core group of friends if you are to reach your support target. This will mean talking to people who may not know you that well, perhaps some who you haven't seen for some time. You will probably also end up talking with people you don't know at all, but who have been introduced to you by someone you do know who has a different network of contacts from you.

Assuming that you've already talked to some of your key close contacts, you might now be getting close to talking to people you don't know that well. These could be people who are a bit lower down the scale in your initial list (remember, your list is supposed to be a dynamic process, not just something you draw up once and then forget; maybe it's time to go back and take a look at who you can contact now that you have covered all your close friends!), or perhaps a friend of a friend, someone you really don't know at all.

The risks – and how to minimise them

With people who you don't know well, you run at least two risks. First of all, because you don't really know their background, **you might simply charge through your presentation without giving them much chance to comment**, turning what should be a relaxed dialogue into an embarrassing monologue. The other risk is the exact opposite. Because the person you are talking to doesn't really know you, **they might lead the conversation down totally irrelevant (to you) tangents**, with no clear way that you can see of getting the discussion back on track again.

In situations like this, it often helps to have some way of **showing** your ministry as well as **talking** about it. It gives you some control over the direction of the conversation and it gives the person you're talking to the confidence that the conversation is going somewhere.

A DVD or other similar presentation can help complement what you say at a group meeting, but it is a bit impersonal for a discussion with an individual or a couple. Having a potential supporter sit looking at a TV screen or, worse still, straining their necks to look at your laptop screen, with a presentation that does all the talking for you isn't really the best way to build a relationship!

☞ You are better having some **visual presentation** that you have prepared yourself: something that is easy to carry round; that acts as a focus for the conversation as opposed to replacing or controlling it; and that gives an overview of the organisation you work with, an outline of your role and the special part that the potential supporter can play.

When we've been working intensively on our support, I've tended to use a **presentation album** for this, the sort with transparent sheets that you can slip pages into.

Remember, this isn't a script. It is simply a visual accompaniment to what you are saying. You might be using this with a Gen X single one day and a couple in their 70s the next, so the content needs to be flexible enough to be useful across a range of ages and types of people.

Elements in a presentation like this include:

- **Highly visual** – lots of pictures, few words
- The **needs** that you or your organisation are addressing; and what are the consequences of these needs?
- What your organisation is doing to **meet these needs** – in broad terms
- Some **specific projects** your organisation is working on, especially in the aspect you will be involved in
- What **your role** is – why you are involved, what you will do, your location, your team etc
- The **supporter's role** – as part of your team; prayers, financial support
- **Ask** – a specific request to the person to be a supporter
- **Thank you** – appreciation expressed

Here's what it might look like:

Let's assume that Jim and Sue Martin had made up a presentation album to explain their proposed work with Declare. The next few pages show what it could look like. Not everybody has the creative or IT skills to make an all-singing-all-dancing presentation. I certainly don't. This example was prepared using Microsoft Word, a scan of a collage of photos, headlines, etc and illustrations that were easily available from the Internet. This isn't meant as a template for you to follow slavishly, but rather an idea of what a simple and basic presentation album could look like.

Remember, the idea of a presentation album is that it illustrates your story and gives a focus to your conversation with a potential supporter. ☞ **From what you already know about Jim and Sue, see if you could tell their story using the presentation album as a base to work from.**

☞ **Now, start drawing out what yours could look like.** It might take you a few attempts before you are happy with it. But, rest assured, it is time well spent.

Initially it might feel a bit strange, even inhibiting, to use a presentation album like this to explain your work and your support needs. ☞ **Practise a few times on a friend until you are comfortable with the flow,** using a couple of different scenarios to prepare for the range of situations in which you are likely to use the album.

Making it Work

**Jim & Sue Martin
Keith and Jenny**

Moving to Stoke to work with

DECLARE!

to help everyone hear the good news of Jesus

Will you join our team?

Overview page

Jesus said, "I am the way the truth and the life." (John 14:6)

60 million people in the UK

Where are they looking?

Who are they listening to?

Less than 5 million go to Church

How will everyone hear the good news of Jesus?

Who can do it?

Don't get stuck listening to travel stories... tell them

WHERE IN THE WORLD?

FOOTBALL'S RICHEST PEOPLE

Wrong answers from wrong places

Wrong messages from wrong people

Paradise remade

LOW PRICE!

A spacious home to boast about!

Need

*These pages are reduced from A4.

Jesus has the answer
(John 14:6)

We need to point to him
(Acts 1:8)

We need to tell 55 million people
(Matt 28:19-20)

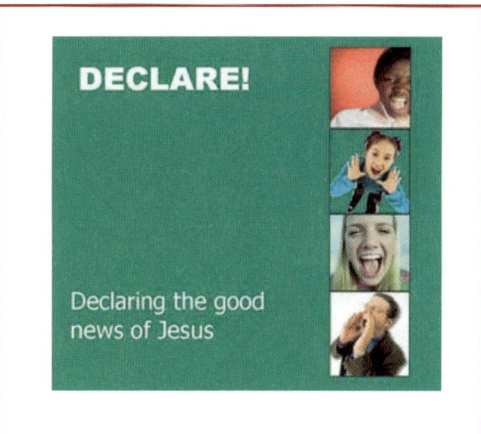

DECLARE!

Declaring the good news of Jesus

DECLARE! is helping make this happen through :

- Equipping churches with resources
- Training in evangelism
- Developing young evangelists

How DECLARE! is addressing the need

DECLARE!

- Started in 1997
- Based in Stoke-on-Trent
- Expanding nationally
- International growth

So far…

- 64 Churches trained in 10 cities
- 15 young evangelists trained last year
- 12 Missions in 5 countries

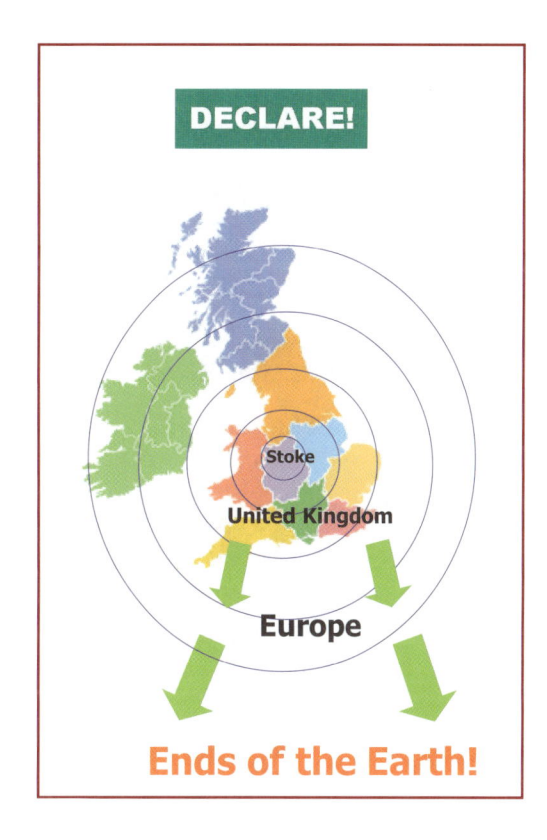

DECLARE!

Stoke
United Kingdom
Europe
Ends of the Earth!

Specific activities of DECLARE!

Making it Work

Why me?

- We also looked in the wrong places for life's answers

- Never been to church

- Didn't really know who Jesus was

- But God chose us!

- Now he's calling me to use my skills to help others hear about Jesus

How can I make a difference?

- Available (redundancy)

- IT and admin skills

- DECLARE! needs to make full use of modern technology to communicate effectively to 55 million people

- Every field evangelist gets the support and resources from the admin office team

It's like getting man into space ......

How Jim fits into the picture

To send up one of these..........

Takes 20 of these......

Over 20 key backroom Mission Control specialists are needed to launch one space shuttle

In the same way DECLARE! field evangelists and trainers need key backroom specialists in IT, admin, accounting ... people like me and you

So where do you come in?

How Jim fits into the picture (contd)

The 20 of these ……….

each have all of these supporting them…………

The 20 specialists in the NASA Mission Control room have 100s of others to call on for support

In the same way you can support my work in DECLARE! as I help ensure that the rest of the staff are equipped to train others to reach the 55 million outside of the church

You can be our support team

What would it involve?

The need for supporters

How can you make a difference?

God has called me to work with DECLARE!

He will provide what we need

We need a team who will:

- Provide financially

- Pray for us

- Encourage us

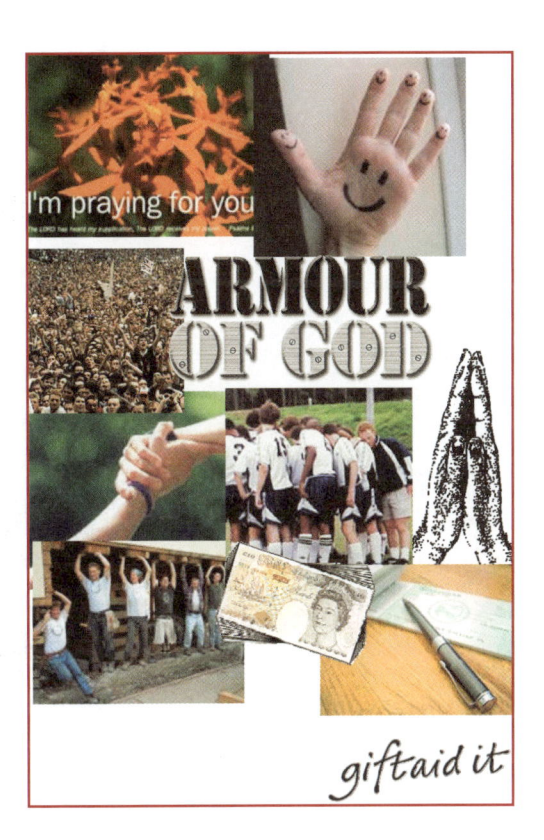

The need for supporters (contd)

Making it Work

Our target.......

To provide for Sue and the children I need a salary of £20,000 per year

Each DECLARE! staff member trusts God to supply their salary through gifts from churches and friends

This could work out like this:

- 4 people giving £100 per month
- 12 people giving £50 per month
- 22 people giving £25 per month
- 15 people giving £10 per month

With Gift Aid DECLARE! can reclaim tax you have paid on your gift!

Right answers from right places

Right messages from right people

Will you help me fulfil God's call to DECLARE! right answers and right messages to others who are listening and looking in the wrong places?

Ask

THANK YOU!

Thank you

CHAPTER 21

RAISING SUPPORT FROM CHURCHES

So far we have concentrated on approaching individuals. What about churches?

A quick look back

In the past, a large amount of mission support came from churches. Missionaries and others in Christian ministry were kept busy with what was called 'deputation', contacting church after church, often those with a historic link to the mission agency, and speaking at meeting after meeting, talking about their work. Sometimes the response was enthusiastic, with the receiving church warmly embracing the work of the organisation represented by the speaker. At other times the response was at best lukewarm, with perhaps a gift that didn't even cover the travel costs of getting to the church.

It was a bit hit and miss, with those churches that showed an active interest in mission tending to get overloaded with requests to come and speak.

Recent decades have seen a big change in this. I suspect that this is at least partly due to the major social changes of the 1960s, which saw a move away from trusting authority structures and institutions towards trusting individual relationships. The 'Baby Boom' generation, who were most affected by this revolution, started choosing to give to people rather than organisations. The past patterns of churches supplying much of the support for Christian organisations were replaced by patterns of individuals supporting people they knew.

The situation today

Whether this direction taken by mission funding is right or wrong (and we could debate that for hours), it is today's reality that people give to people more than churches give to organisations. And this pattern shows no sign of changing. The generations following the Baby Boomers still prefer to relate to people rather than to institutions.

It is also the case that mission and ministry in the 21st century are much more diverse, complex and expensive than in previous eras. In our own church, for example, with a membership of fewer than 200, we have nine couples and three singles who live on a variety of support systems and who look to us, to some extent, as their sending church. There is simply no way that we could cover the full cost of all these great people. Our missions committee has worked out a way of dividing up the available money between the various people, but it doesn't even come close to covering their real needs. To help bridge the gap, we actively encourage our missionaries to raise as much support as they can from individuals, both those in our church and elsewhere.

Bearing all this in mind, it is not abnormal today for someone to have up to 80 per cent of their support coming from individuals and 20 per cent from church budgets.

But support from churches still needs to play a vital part for anyone raising support for Christian ministry. Churches constantly need to have opportunities to stretch their vision beyond their immediate and local ministries. Individuals raising support need the commitment of a body of people who can corporately offer the finances, prayers and encouragement in a way that individuals cannot.

Being multi-churched

Most people will have a number of different types of church relationships, ranging from the one they count as their present spiritual home, to the one they got invited to speak at because a friend from work goes there. Clearly the key relationship is with the home – or sending – church. But that might not always be as straightforward as it seems.

Let's take another look at Claire and Jim and Sue.

For Jim and Sue, it is easy. They have only ever been members of one church – Thomas Avenue Baptist Church in Leicester. They became Christians eight years ago through the witness of Ken, a work colleague of Jim's, who was a member there. It was the obvious thing to go to the same church as Ken. In fact, they never even considered looking at other churches. As total novices at church life, it was scary enough for them to get used to just one!

Claire, however, has four churches she would count as 'home' churches.

First of all there is St James' on the outskirts of Newcastle where she grew up and where her parents still attend. It was here that Claire made her commitment to Christ as a child and also where she first got excited about mission through the church's contacts with a dynamic Church Missionary Society missionary in Uganda. Then there is Westside Community Church in Liverpool where she went during her student days. It was here that Claire really started to take an active part in church life, involved in everything from the worship group to a late-night outreach in the night-club area of the city.

In Sheffield she first went to St Phillip's for a few years, helping with the Alpha courses and being part of the missions committee. Two years ago, with about 40 others, she moved to Newgrove Church Centre, a daughter church of St Phillip's that was being set up in a new housing area closer to where Claire lives. Claire is part of the leadership team at Newgrove. If pushed to make a choice, Claire would say that St Phillip's is still her spiritual home, but she would rather not have to make that choice, because all four are important to her.

Most people today have more than one church where they have been fed spiritually, where they are known and from which they could reasonably expect to receive some support. But, in the end, there is usually one that comes top of the pile, the church that you'd call your spiritual home.

So how does it all work?

What are the rules for approaching a church for support?

Churches, like people, differ from each other. In Claire's case, what might work in St James' may not work at all in Westside Community Church, and St Phillip's might require a different approach again.

With individuals, it is relatively easy for you to set the agenda. Most individuals are not all that organised in their giving, so if you offer the option of giving monthly by standing order, that's what they're likely to do. They are also often quite willing for you to suggest an amount or a range that they should consider giving. They simply don't know the rules, so they are quite comfortable with you giving them guidelines. Also, individuals are giving from the resources under their direct control.

A church, on the other hand, is giving money that has been entrusted to it by the giving of its members. Decisions about where the money goes are made on behalf of the whole church, not just at the whim of those making the decision. So there are usually rules, or guidelines, in place. Sometimes they are well thought through and clearly stated. At other times they are a bit ad hoc, perhaps even contradictory, and unclear. But there are always rules of some sort and, while you might be tempted to bend them as far as you can, you can't break them!

Below are a few key pointers to working with your home church in your journey into Christian ministry.

Early warning

☞ **Make sure that you talk to someone in your church leadership about your thoughts about going into Christian ministry right at the beginning.** It doesn't help your cause if the first thing your church leader knows about your plans is when he gets a reference to complete from a Christian organisation you're planning to join or Bible college you hope to attend. It isn't fair on a church to expect them to automatically endorse and fund a decision in which they really had no part.

Oops, too late!

If you're already well down the line and haven't really talked through your decision with your church, then maybe some damage limitation is called for. There is an old Chinese proverb that goes something like this: *"When is the best time to plant a tree? Thirty years ago. But if you didn't plant it thirty years ago, plant it today."* So, if you didn't talk through your desire to go into Christian ministry at the outset, contact someone in your church's leadership today, say that you realise you probably should have talked things through earlier, and ask for their thoughts and input now.

Learn the rules

☞ **Find out if your church has any set guidelines for its missions giving.** Ideally, you want to have someone who is involved in the process, but who is also acting on your behalf – maybe a member of the mission committee who you know quite well. I've listed some of the general issues you need to check out. There are probably other issues that are specific to your situation that you can think of. If so, add them to the end of the list.

- Is the church already supporting other missionaries?
- Is there a church mission budget?
- If so, how are decisions made about allocating this?
- If not, and the church already supports others, how does this work?
- Who makes these decisions?
- Is it OK to approach individuals in the church who you know for support?
- How do you go about applying for funding from the church itself?
- What information does the church need in order to make a decision about supporting you and the level of support they might give?
- Would it help to have someone from the organisation you are joining contact the church to discuss the financial policies of the organisation?

- What are the church's expectations of those they support financially?
-
-
-

Start talking

As soon as you have been accepted by your organisation, ☞ **start talking about what you hope to do**. You don't have to have all the details worked out. There still might be some uncertainty about what your assignment will be; it might not be clear yet if you'll be going in the spring or summer; there might still be some questions about whether you need some additional training. It doesn't matter. You should have enough information to begin getting people used to the fact that you're on your way. And you need to let people know the passion of your heart – that is always more important than the fine-tuned details of the job anyway.

As far as you are able, ☞ **get to talk to house groups, midweek groups, youth groups** and any other aspect of your church's life that will give you an airing. ☞ **And see if you can get a slot on a Sunday morning**. Even if it is just a short interview for a couple of minutes, not only does it let the majority of the church know that something is happening, it also demonstrates an endorsement of your decision by the church leadership.

☞ The purpose of all this isn't to raise support. It is to let as many people as possible know as soon as possible that big changes are underway in your life. You should, of course, mention that you will be raising support for your new work, but this is an information process, not a solicitation process. That will come over cups of coffee with individuals in the following weeks and months.

Build the family

Your church is most likely to be the main expression of God's family in your life. As you get ready for whatever God has in store for you, it is important to make sure that you build up a strong partnership with your church. It isn't so much that you are going with their backing. **It is more that your church is going and that you are the family member representing them.** Even if they have limited experience, or even limited interest, in sending missionaries, you should do the best job you can at communicating the importance of what Paul called *"your partnership in the gospel from the first day until now"* when he wrote to his supporting church in Philippi. If there is ever a breakdown in communication, or unfulfilled expectations, try to ensure that the fault doesn't lie at your door.

Look beyond the obvious

Yes, your friends are likely to want to support you. So will some of the real 'mission keenies' in the church.

But who are you forgetting?

Think through the various groups and ages in the church. How can being connected to you and your work help develop a wider vision in these various aspects of church life? Give special attention to children and teenagers in the church. They may not be able to be of any significant help to you financially, but if you can inspire them with stories of lives changed through creative ministry, then they might just want to follow you into some type of Christian ministry themselves. Christian young people are in desperate need of Holy Heroes as role models – you can be just that.

Appoint an Ambassador

Unless you are raising support to work in your immediate home area and intend staying in your church, you will end up some distance away from your sending church. In Jim and Sue's case, although they are only moving to Stoke, as they get more involved in a church there they will have less and less opportunity to get back to Leicester. Claire certainly won't get the chance to pop back from Turkey to Sheffield (or Liverpool or Newcastle for that matter) at the drop of a hat.

Inevitably, your links with the church will get weaker over the years. Yes, some links with individuals will get stronger as they become an important part of your support team, but your contact with the overall church will decline. The changes may be small and almost imperceptible for those there all the time. But new members joining, others moving on, some people with changed interests, new appointments to leadership roles all combine to make the church you will come back to visit a different church from the one you left.

To keep your profile up during your absence, **get someone in the church to act as your link with the rest of the congregation.** I don't mean someone who will just put out your prayer letters at the back. I mean someone with enough initiative to make sure that your name gets mentioned in the right places at the right time. Whether they are phoning the minister on a Thursday evening to say that they've just got an email from you and that you've got a bad tummy bug (or whatever) and asking if you can get a special mention in the prayers on Sunday, or getting a note about some news from you in the church newsletter, or suggesting that a few people go to visit you in the summer, they are making sure that you and your ministry remain a constant in the changing face of your church.

All this, of course, means that you will need to keep up regular contact with this link person. They can only put out what you put in.

Book the spare bed

No matter how good you are at telling your story, no matter how committed people in your church are to supporting you, their lives and yours are lived out in very different contexts. Without actually seeing your context, without getting to experience some of what you experience, you will always have an uphill struggle to get people to understand fully this new life that you are embarking on.

☞ **Right from the outset, try to get people thinking about coming to visit you.** Whether it is someone popping up for an evening from Leicester to Stoke so that Jim and Sue can show them around the Declare office or bring them along to some ministry event in the area, or someone taking a week of their holidays to visit Claire in Turkey, nothing helps promote you back in your own church like an enthusiast who has been there. And if someone from your church leadership comes, even better.

Other churches

Most people will have some contact with churches beyond their home church. While some will be easy to identify and contact, like Claire's church connections in Newcastle and Liverpool, others may take more creative thought and work. As with all support-raising, you are really only likely to succeed if there is some personal contact. Church treasurers are not sitting around wishing that missionaries who they don't know and have never heard of would show up so that they can give away all the church's surplus funds. If you do find churches like this, please let me know where they are!

But you probably do have contacts in other churches that might be worth exploring.

Jim and Sue

Take Jim and Sue's situation. Ken, Jim's work colleague who was so influential in their commitment to Christ eight years ago, was made redundant along with Jim two years ago. He couldn't find work locally but did get a job in Manchester, which is where his wife, Sarah, is from originally. It doesn't pay as well as his previous job, but they get by OK. They moved to Manchester 18 months ago, just before Jim went to Bible College for a year.

They have followed Jim and Sue's progress with great interest, meeting up a few times during the past 18 months. Ken and Sarah gave a sizable gift out of their redundancy money to help Jim's Bible College costs and they were also among the first to offer to support Jim and Sue for their work with Declare. At £40 per month, it's not as much as they'd have liked to have given, but it's as much as they can stretch to just now.

By now, of course, Ken and Sarah are involved in a church in Manchester. They are in a house group, have made some good friends and have got involved in a few different aspects of church life.

Although Jim and Sue think that they have only one set of Christian friends – those in their own church – if they stopped to think about it, they have more contacts in other places than they realise.

People like Ken and Sarah can offer introductions to their friends, house group and to their whole church. Ken and Sarah might well have other Christian contacts in Manchester, work colleagues, Sarah's family, etc who might be in other churches still, giving a much wider scope for potential support than Jim and Sue would ever have realised.

"OK," says Jim, *"there might be other people out there in other churches, but they're friends of friends. We don't know them ourselves. Why would they support us?"*

I don't know. And, until he tries, Jim doesn't know either.

'Third party' supporters

What I do know is that most people who raise support have supporters who they didn't know at all before they started raising support. The support comes for a variety of reasons and the relationships that grow out of these 'third party' supporters can sometimes be stronger than the relationships with the original contacts. It isn't logical. **But the whole process isn't based on logic. It is based on God bringing together two sets of people, one with a need to give and the other with a need to receive.** Sometimes, whether or not they knew each other in the past is irrelevant. After all, some of those on the team you will be working with are people you didn't know before. Why should it be any different with the team of people who support you?

Most of these introductions will lead to individual supporters, but a few will also lead you to possible church support or support from some aspect of a church where your contact has some input – a youth group, women's study group, house group or whatever. Always be looking for opportunities to take the relationship to the next stage. You might be much more pleasantly surprised than you expect.

A word of advice here. **It is important to have your original contact on board as a supporter before they introduce you to others.** This adds a huge amount of credibility to the introduction. It wouldn't make a lot of sense, for example, for Ken and Sarah to introduce Jim and Sue to their home group with the expectation of some members in the group supporting them if Ken and Sarah haven't already signed up.

In the next chapter we'll look at what do to with the sort of meeting that can be set up by a supporter to introduce you to their friends.

☞ **Take a few minutes to think about Christians you know who have a different network of contacts from yours.** These could be:

- people from your past who live in a totally different part of the country
- former members of your church who have moved away
- people who have moved to your church in recent years from another part of the country
- work colleagues who are in a different church
- family members in different parts of the country.

As long as your relationship is, or was, strong enough for you to give them a call to talk about it, then you should go ahead and give them that call.

☞ **Use the page opposite or a blank sheet to see where these contacts might take you.**

> George was leaving a well-paid job in the insurance industry to join an organisation that specialises in ministry to families. He had approached Richard, a Christian business contact, to ask if he could support him. Although Richard appeared positive about George's move, he said that he just wasn't in a position to support him financially at this time.
>
> They kept in touch a bit in the following months and when Richard realised that George still had some way to go to reach his support target, he suggested that George come and speak to his church house group. He assured George that there were some wealthy people in the group.
>
> As graciously as he could, George told Richard that it really wouldn't work. Richard was trying to encourage others to do what he himself wasn't doing – give financial support to George. It didn't matter how much Richard gave, George explained, but it would be important for Richard to have made a support commitment himself before introducing George to his friends.
>
> Richard saw the sense in this and agreed that he would need to give something. You can imagine George's shock when Richard said, "But I'm afraid I can only give £100 per month".
>
> I wonder what Richard thought was 'normal' to give?

Throwing the net wider

List below the contacts you have whose own network of contacts are significantly different from yours. Your starting point might be an individual, a group of some sort, or a church.

List as much information as you can and begin building a plan to see where these contacts might lead to. You will be surprised what names come to mind as you work on this.

I've filled in a line that Jim and Sue might have completed for Ken and Sarah to give you an idea of how this could look.

Name	**Relationship**	**Possible introductions**	**Next steps**
Ken and Sarah	Good friends + monthly supporters	• Their house group • Friends in their church • Their church • Other friends • Sarah's family	Call Ken to arrange meeting up to talk about this

Notes

CHAPTER 22

MEETINGS

Generally, meetings are not the best places to ask for support, but they can be a great way to give information. They can also help surface those who might be interested in supporting you.

There tend to be two types of meetings where you will get to speak about your work:

- regular meetings where you are given a slot to speak
- meetings specially set up for you to talk about your work.

Let's look at them both in some detail.

A regular meeting where you are given a slot

At meetings of groups who meet regularly, you may be given anything from a few minutes during a Sunday morning service to a whole evening at a house group. Or you may be speaking at the midweek service, the ladies' fellowship, the missionary prayer meeting, or any other type of meeting that is part of the existing church programme.

What all these meetings have in common is that most of those present haven't come especially to hear you. They are there because they always go to that meeting. This is a good time to stir up interest, but not to ask directly for support. You can, of course, ask people who are interested to speak to you afterwards, maybe even pass out a brochure about your proposed work and your financial support needs to everyone present.

Immediately after the meeting, some people might express serious interest in supporting you – ☞ **always have copies of your standing order form and Gift Aid Declaration form with you, just in case.**

On the other hand, you might also find that the support-raising version of Murphy's Law kicks in. This is when the person who can be of least help to you monopolises your time so that others who would like to speak to you can't get to you. It's the man who comes up after you've spoken, full of praise for what you've said and mentions that his cousin once worked with Mid Med Mission in Peru. No, he recalls it was Mid Andes Mission. Does Mid Med Mission work in Peru too?, No, you assure him, Mid Med Mission doesn't work in Peru. So you won't need to learn Spanish, then, he persists. No, you won't need to learn Spanish. His cousin was fluent. And so the conversation goes.

This is probably all very important to the person who approached you, and you should recognise it as such. But it's not a lot of help to you when three different couples who wanted to talk to you about your support have to leave to go home before you eventually get away from the Peru discussion.

☞ **All the more important at least to get some sort of brochure with a response page into people's hands.** The really keen ones just might get round to filling it in or getting back to you afterwards.

A few guidelines about regular meetings:

- Know what the purpose of the meeting is and fit in with this.
- Well in advance of the meeting, ask whoever is in charge if you can mention your support and if you can hand out information.
- Ask how long you have to speak; if they say to take as long as you want, ask again – they don't mean it!
- Get there early enough to see what it feels like to stand where you'll be speaking from.
- If you have a video or DVD you want to show as part of the presentation, check that all the necessary equipment is available and try it out before people arrive. If you can't get it to work by the time the meeting is due to start, go ahead without it.
- Tailor what you say to the nature of the meeting, how long you have been given to speak and what you want to achieve from this particular meeting.
- Know how to finish. Have your last sentence well rehearsed so that you don't end by drifting off vaguely into the horizon.
- What you want to say and what they need to hear are not always the same thing. Five minutes of key people-stories that illustrate the needs you or your organisation are addressing and how you plan to address those needs will beat 20 minutes of complex detail.

- Practise, especially if you are not used to public speaking. Stand in front of a mirror and give your talk out loud. If you have a couple of friends who can be guinea pigs for your rehearsals, even better.
- Keep good eye contact with people. If you are showing images on a screen behind you while you are speaking, don't talk when your head is turned looking at the screen.
- Acknowledge, educate, involve: thank them for the chance to speak, tell them what your plans are, tell them how they can help.

A special meeting to hear about your work

This type of meeting is typically arranged by a friend who has a different network of contacts from yours as an opportunity for you to explain about your work to their friends. It is the sort of event that Ken and Sarah might arrange for Jim and Sue.

It could be in a home with anywhere between six and 20 people showing up.

Before looking at what to do in a meeting like this, a couple of background comments:

1. There is a temptation to organise a meeting like this for your own friends, the people you see from time to time anyway. Surely it would make sense and save time by explaining your work to everyone at one go? And it also feels a lot more comfortable than speaking to people on their own.

    Don't do it!

    Your friends need to be treated as individuals, not as part of a group. And remember, if you try to avoid the discomfort of speaking to them personally, it may well transfer to the potential supporter. In this case, it could leave some of your close friends feeling that you're treating them too impersonally for the level of your friendship. Queen Victoria once said of Disraeli, *"He addresses me as though I were a public meeting!"* Don't fall into the same trap with your friends.

2. There's also an issue about your host for the evening.

    Remember, the only link you have with the guests that evening is through your mutual friend. As I've already explained, this person should already be supporting you. He or she can say this as they introduce you, which immediately enhances your credibility with the others.

Let's assume that you contact a friend in some far-flung part of the country to ask if you can come and talk about the possibility of them supporting you. It will mean an overnight stay and, to maximise your visit, your friend suggests getting some friends together that evening so that you can talk to them all.

Again, it sounds good. But you'd be better advised explaining that it is him (or her, or them) in particular that you want to come and talk to and that maybe at some later date you could come back if they'd like to organise a group. It will be well worth the double visit, especially for your friend who, in the first instance, realises that you're not just out chasing any money you can find but that you would particularly like them on your support team. Assuming that they do agree to support you, then when you go back to speak to a group they've organised for you, your friend is then clearly acting on your behalf, almost as your agent, standing with you and encouraging others to take the same step they have taken. Much more effective.

But, back to the special meeting organised by your friend. The difference between this and a regular meeting is that you are the only reason the meeting is being held. If you had to cancel at the last minute, the meeting wouldn't happen. In a context like this you can be as open as you want about your support – that's what they've come to hear about.

When you are making the arrangements with the host, ☞ **check with him who he plans to invite**. If, for example, half the missions committee from his church will be there, you can assume an existing keen interest in mission. If, on the other hand, he's inviting the church's Thursday evening five-a-side football team, the flavour of the evening might be a bit different!

Also, ☞ **make sure he tells his friends that you will be talking about your work *and* about your support needs**. You don't want any surprises on the night, either for you or for the guests.

☞ **Think carefully before using any video/DVD presentation in a context like this.** It can be a help, but if you are all squeezed into a friend's lounge, there might not be the room you need to make it work. Decide before you start rather than simply go ahead and show it without thinking. These days DVDs are so cheap to reproduce that you could give each person or couple a copy to take home with them as a souvenir of the evening.

☞ **It's probably best to have your bit at the start of the evening**, then have a cup of coffee at the end, but take your host's advice about what would work best for this group.

At the start of the evening ☞ **have the host introduce you**, with a brief comment about how you know each other and also saying that he or she is already committed to supporting you.

Then it's over to you

- All you need to do is **follow the same sort of flow as you would with a friend, but with a bit more background about yourself**, given that these people don't know you.

- The less people know you, the more important it is to **use people-stories**. Even if they have no knowledge of you or your background, they'll be able to relate to stories about people whose needs are being met through the type of work that you'll be doing.

- Assuming that the group is small enough, this is the sort of situation where a **presentation album** can be a great help – and a good reason to have the album highly visual, with few words and these as large as you can get them. You don't want to ruin people's eyesight by having them squint at impossibly small writing.

See pages 200–204

- If you have chosen to have a DVD or video, either about your work in particular or the mission in general, make sure that you use it to add to what you say, not replace it. In many cases, the people at the meeting will not know you. The sound of your own voice, and the passion with which you talk about what God has called you to, will give people a glimpse of the real you much more than a video or DVD. Yes, by all means, use good media material to illustrate what you say, but it needs to be exactly that: illustrating what you say. That's where the presentation album works best – it supplies the visuals and some of the headline words; you supply the voice.

- Whether or not you use a presentation album, at the end you need to do **a simple ask**. They have come expecting to hear someone involved in some aspect of Christian ministry talk about their work and about their support needs – don't disappoint them!

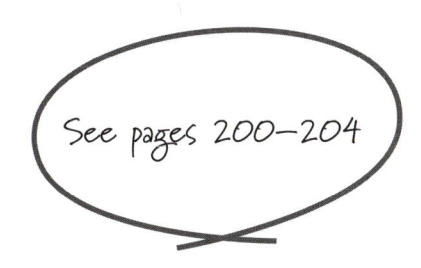

Example: Claire

Let's look at how Claire could end a presentation she is doing to a group back in Westside Community Church in Liverpool. One of her old student friends stayed on in Liverpool after college and has asked Claire back to speak to some people who she feels might be interested in hearing about her work in Turkey. Claire has used a presentation album to explain her work and is still using it as she talks about her support needs.

Here's what the ending might sound like

"As you can imagine, this isn't the sort of work I can do on my own. I've already met a couple of the team that I'll be joining in Turkey and, from what I've seen, I couldn't ask for a better bunch of people to work with. Their experience and maturity will be important for me, especially in my first couple of years.

But there's another team that I need to make this all become a reality. And that's a team back here in Britain.

The way Mid Med Mission works is that each staff member builds around them a group of people who will support them through regular financial support, regular prayer and regular encouragement.

I need the financial support because that is the only source of income I'll have. So far I've been very encouraged by the response from people I've talked to and I've got just over 60 per cent of my support raised.

I need prayers because the work will be a spiritual battleground. For the most part, the Kurdish people haven't rejected Jesus – they simply have never had the chance to say 'yes' to him. As you can imagine, Satan wants to keep it that way. I see teaching English as not just giving people a language that they are very keen to learn, although that has value in its own right. I also see it as a way of building bridges with people, especially people who want to see something different in their lives.

It will give me the credibility in the community to allow me also to communicate God's love into their lives. And if you can influence the influencers in Kurdish society, it can have a ripple effect for the gospel throughout whole communities.

It won't be easy. If it was, it would have been done years ago. But your prayers can make the difference and can help see a spiritual breakthrough for the gospel among people who have never really had the chance to hear the gospel in a way they can understand.

I need encouragement because I know it will be a challenge to adapt to a new culture, learn a new language, be the new guy in a team of missionaries, take on new responsibilities and all the other aspects of living and working among Kurdish people that I haven't even thought of.

Don't get me wrong – I'm really looking forward to it and I know that this is where God wants me. But I am sure that there will be times of doubt and frustration. I'll need to know that there are people back here who are my encouragers. People who will urge me to keep going and to fulfil all that God has in store for my life."

What happens when you stop speaking?

At this stage you hit a problem. Among those who have listened patiently to you for the past 15 minutes or so are a few who aren't really all that interested; others with some interest but who don't plan to offer much response; and a key group whose interest is sufficient for them to want to support you. But, short of a large dose of the gift of discernment, you don't know who's at what level of interest among the smiling faces in front of you.

For example, if Claire simply left it open-ended with a comment like, *"So, if you'd like to be part of my support team to bring God's love to the Kurdish people of eastern Turkey, please do speak to me afterwards"* she can be almost guaranteed that the Murphy's Law I described earlier will kick in.

And she can't say, *"Thank you for listening. All those interested in supporting me, please put your hand up. We'll sing another verse of Just as I Am while you make up your mind. The buses will wait!"*

So how do you find out who is interested without causing embarrassment and without losing them?

What I've found helpful is ☞ **to pass out simple lined index cards to everyone as you finish speaking.**

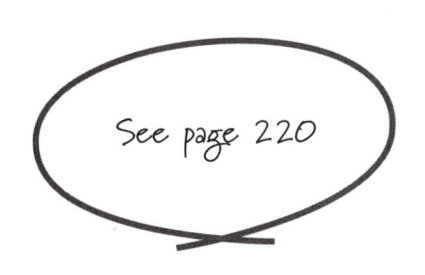

(See page 220)

Claire could say something like:

"I hope that what you've heard tonight has been an encouragement to you. I know that I've certainly been encouraged by you being here. I'd like to keep in touch with you and let you know what God is doing among the Kurdish people I'll be working with. Please put your name, address, phone number and email address on the card and I'll keep in touch a few times a year over the next couple of years.

I'd also like to ask you to give serious thought to becoming part of my support team as I head off to Turkey. As I said earlier, I can't – and dare not – go without a group of people committed to being my team back here who will give, pray and encourage.

If, as a result of what you've heard tonight, you'd like to talk further about being part of my support team, please put a tick on the card and I'll get back to you. You can either hand your card to me or leave it on the table by the door. Thank you."

This way, those who are interested in supporting you can let you know of their interest without embarrassment, because the others with less interest will also be writing their details on their cards. For those who put a ✓ on their card, **give them a call within 48 hours at the most to thank them for their interest and to arrange to meet them to talk more about your support.** For the others, simply add them to your prayer-letter list. Who knows what might come out of their contact with you in the coming couple of years.

In our early years of raising support, we had quite a few support evenings like this. However, until we worked out a simple way of people letting us know that they were interested in supporting us, I'm sure that we lost many potential supporters – people who would have been willing to talk further about supporting us, but who didn't quite get to let us know on the night. Yes, a few did persist but, when compared with the much higher number of those signing up once we started using the index card response idea, I'm sure that we lost many more than we gained.

CHAPTER 23

WHEN THE WELL RUNS DRY

It happens to almost everybody when they are raising support. They run out of names. **At least they think they have run out of names.** They begin to get discouraged. The earlier momentum of support-raising has slowed down, even stopped. They can't think of anyone else to contact. The contacts well has run dry.

Maybe you'll never reach the bottom of your contacts well. Or perhaps you might in the coming weeks and months. But, let's assume you have already hit the bottom. What now?

Remember Elijah

First of all, there are almost 60 million people living in the UK. You can't, surely, have talked to all of them? OK, let's just limit it to active Christians – those with a living faith who are likely to be those interested in Christian ministry and mission. How many would that be? Even if it is only three per cent of the population, that's still close to two million people. Yes, I know that you only know a few of these personally. But God knows them all and he will have plans to bring some of them across your path.

Remember when Elijah got downhearted when his plans began to unravel? ☞ **Take a few minutes and read the story again in 1 KINGS 19.** Elijah thought that there was no one else who would join him. He felt downhearted and despairing. He had reached the bottom of his well. He thought that there was nothing more he could do, nowhere else he could go. He was so discouraged that he hid away where no one would get to him. When God asked him what he was doing, hiding away, Elijah trotted out all his woes, that there was no one left who understood what he was trying to do and no one left who would stand with him.

What did God do? He spoke to Elijah in a gentle whisper, assuring him that there were 7,000 others who were part of his plan. Of course Elijah would not have known who all these 7,000 were, but it was good to be assured by God that they were there.

What did God ask Elijah to do next? He didn't send him off in a new direction. No, **he asked Elijah to retrace his steps**, back down a road he had already travelled [v.15], where he thought that there was no one who would join him. It was here that he would find those God had chosen to go with him. God also told him to start out by contacting three people, not all 7,000.

So Elijah went back down the road and met up with Elisha, one of the three, who was more than eager to act as an attendant, or supporter, to Elijah. This was on a road that Elijah had travelled previously, but he had somehow missed Elisha first time round. This time, looking with different eyes, he saw what God saw – Elisha just waiting to be asked to join up.

☞ If you have really got stuck and are hiding away – metaphorically, if not literally – thinking that there is no one left for you to contact, maybe you need to have a serious talk to God about it. Pour out all your woes, but then listen to his gentle whisper, assuring you that he has his people out there, ready to stand with you. Like Elijah, it might well mean going back over ground you've already tried, but this time looking with God's eyes, seeing what you missed the last time.

They are out there, maybe not 7,000, but certainly enough to meet all your needs. Start looking at the process with different eyes. Realise that God has already provided the supporters you need. You simply have to find them – and they may not be where you expected. Find your Elisha, someone who would be more than willing to be a supporter, but who hasn't had the chance yet to say yes. And then move on to the next, and the next.

Retracing your steps

The following pages give a few ideas to get you started back down the road already travelled.

1 Clear up loose ends

As you go through the process, there will inevitably be some loose ends that need to be chased up. For example, those who have agreed to support you but haven't completed the necessary forms. Get back to these people to clarify their situation. Yes, you can list reasons why this will be difficult: it's been too long ago; if they were really interested they would have called me; I don't want to appear pushy.

But among these people will be some of those who God has brought across your path, whether to fulfil a need in their lives or in yours, or both. Maybe they seemed obvious potential supporters to you at the time, but it has all got a bit lost, just because of some loose ends.

Give them a call, offering an apology if you need to because of the time gap in getting back to them, and ask if they have had any further thoughts about supporting you. Tell them that you realise that there are a few people that you haven't got back to and that, if you could clarify their situation, it would help you know how close you are to your support target.

After this renewed contact there might well be some more loose ends to clear up. For example, they might have lost the original standing order form and you need to get another one to them. This time, make sure that you follow through until the deal is done.

☞ **Take time now and go back over the contacts you've already had, but where there is still some unfinished business.**

- Write down their names and, as far as you remember it, where the support discussion has got to.
- What hasn't been done that needs to be done?
- Can you identify a blockage?
- What do you need to do next to get the process back on track?

Once you've got some idea of what needs to be done, ☞ **get on and do it**. Yes, you'll probably feel a bit uncomfortable, especially if you're not exactly sure what the state of play is with a particular individual. Even if the person chooses not to support you, at least you've clarified the situation and can move on.

But a good many will sign up – all they need is for you to pick up the loose ends and help them tie them up.

2 The forgotten excluded

Supporters come in all shapes and sizes, including the clearly obvious and the totally unexpected. They don't carry signs saying 'I'm a potential supporter, please ask me'. If they did it would make our job a lot easier! We would also get plenty of surprises at who were holding the signs – and also who weren't.

But as they are not that easy to spot, sometimes they slip through the cracks because we're not looking with the right eyes. We can think that if we've contacted all the obvious ones – the house group members, other friends from church, a few work colleagues and some family members – then there's no one left.

But, like the iceberg, what you see on the surface is only part of the story, and it might just be a small part.

☞ **Sit down and take stock.** Who have you not approached who is still lurking in the back of your mind, or maybe at the bottom of the list you drew up right at the start of your support-raising? Maybe it is someone who hasn't been in touch with you for years. It might be someone you really don't know that well. Or perhaps someone who doesn't have much money. Maybe someone who you think is already over-committed supporting other missionaries.

By not giving these people at least the chance to say 'no' themselves, then you are saying 'no' on their behalf. What if they'd like to say 'yes'?

☞ **Leave aside all the reasons why you haven't contacted them before.** Start looking at it with different eyes.

That old college friend who was so helpful to you when you went through a crisis of faith during your student days. Just because your only contact for a few years has been at Christmas card level, does that mean they wouldn't be interested? Come to think of it, they might well be delighted to hear of your plans and even be a bit miffed if you didn't give them the chance to be part of your future.

Or the old couple in your church who don't have much money. Who said that it is only those with obvious spare disposable income who can be supporters?

☞ **Be careful about pre-judging people's response.** That's what prejudice is: a pre-judgement. How would you like it if people pre-judged you and cut you out of opportunities to give, just because they thought you couldn't afford it because you are living on a support basis?

Don't deny others the chance at least to say 'no' for themselves.

☞ **Take time now and list those you've chosen not to approach.** Think hard and don't exclude anyone at this stage.

☞ **Then go back over your list and ask yourself if you have excluded any of these just because of your own feelings.** Have you pre-judged their response simply because you are over-cautious about approaching them?

If you're still not sure, try this:

- Reverse the roles. If you were the person who might be able to support someone on your list and they were going into some type of support-dependent Christian ministry, would you want to know?
- How would you feel if they asked you to consider being part of their support team?
- And how would you feel if they didn't and you found out that they had deliberately chosen not to ask you?
- My guess is that there are at least some on your list who you would have no problem being approached by in these circumstances, whether or not you were able to help them financially.
- Switch back again. You are the one with the unusual plans for your future and needing support to see these plans fulfilled. Recognise that the blockage is with you and how you feel, not with them.

☞ **So, take the plunge. Give them a call, have a chat with them or drop them a note. Remember, it is more blessed to give than to receive, but it is a lot more difficult to receive than to give!**

David had been working as an evangelist for years, helping churches the length and breadth of the country to reach out with the gospel to their communities.

Mr and Mrs Thompson had started supporting David almost at the beginning of his ministry. Now, years later, Mr Thompson had died and Mrs Thompson was getting quite frail and was living in sheltered accommodation. Although her income was a lot less

> *than it had been in the past, Mrs Thompson had still maintained the same monthly support for David as she and her husband had been giving when their finances were a lot stronger.*
>
> *Assuming that Mrs Thompson was too embarrassed to stop the support which he felt she could no longer really afford, he called to see her one day and explained that she had done her bit over the years and that if she needed to stop her support now, it was OK.*
>
> *Mrs Thompson started to cry. "Don't stop me now," she said. "Please don't stop me now. All I have left are the four walls of this room. I don't get out much and can't really do much anymore. But by supporting you I'm still telling people about Jesus."*

David had almost stopped what had become an increasingly important part of Mrs Thompson's life. Be careful about your pre-judgements. Mrs Thompson kept supporting David until the day she went to glory.

3 Who's new to you?

See page 142

If you've followed this workbook through from the beginning, you will have come up with a list of Christians who you know or who know you. That was a snapshot of your contacts network at that time. Even if you didn't compile a list, as you have been working on your support you have probably been contacting people on the basis of a relationship that you have had with them for some time.

But what about those you've just met recently? How long do you need to know someone before they should be allowed to support you? And who says so?

See page 78

Just because you don't know someone that well doesn't mean that you shouldn't consider asking them to support you. Remember, this process is as much, if not more, about meeting needs in their lives as it is in providing you with money. Take off the blinkers that can so easily restrict our view and start looking for possibilities in a new contact, not restrictions. ☞ **Re-read the story of Elaine meeting Sandra on the bus.**

If it was all about you and how you feel, then maybe there would be reasons not to approach some of your most recent contacts. But it is also about the other person and their unmet needs. At least explore it a bit and see what happens.

A couple in our church work many miles from home and only get back to us every so often. I've noticed that during these infrequent visits home they work hard at getting to know the new people in the church, people they haven't met before. You never know when something unusual comes out of a brand new relationship.

☞ **Take some time and review who you have met for the first time in the past month.** Maybe it was someone new in church. Perhaps a friend or family member of someone you know from work. Or someone you sat beside at some event. Who are they? What was the context in which you met them? Was there anything in your conversation with them about your plans?

Leaving aside the fact that you don't know them well and have just recently met them, is there any other reason why you shouldn't approach them about supporting you?

Precisely because there is no previous history to complicate the relationship, it can sometimes be even easier to approach these brand new contacts. Their initial introduction to you probably included some reference to your plans for the future, so that's where they are starting from. ☞ **Build on this, keeping it casual and informal.**

Example: Jim

The contact will, of course, differ from person to person, but let's set an imaginary phone call for Jim with Chris, who he'd met at the home of John, a mutual friend from Jim's church. This could be what it sounds like from Jim's side of the conversation:

"Chris, this is Jim Martin. We met at John's the other night? It was good to meet somebody else who had become a Christian later in life. So many of the others in the church come from Christian backgrounds and I'm not sure if they always understand what it feels like coming in from the outside.

Look, the reason I'm calling is that, as I mentioned, we're moving to Stoke in the new year to work with Declare. Declare do a great job helping churches reach out to people who have no church background at all. I'll be looking after their admin and keeping all the IT bits of the organisation working. John thought you might be interested in hearing about our work and suggested that I give you a call.

Right now I'm building a support team for my work with Declare, people with a heart for bringing the gospel to the unchurched and who might be interested in supporting us financially in our work. Because you came through this long road into Christian faith just like we did, I was wondering if you'd like to meet up for a chat to learn more about our plans and maybe how you could be part of it as a supporter?"

Now that wasn't too difficult was it? It was casual enough for Chris to back off with no offence given or taken. It was building on their existing contact, recent and brief as it was. It also got to the point quickly, otherwise Chris would be wondering why on earth Jim was phoning him. In this case, it also built on their mutual relationship with John.

Your situation will be different from Jim's, but using the sort of approach that Jim used with Chris, who is there who you have only recently met who you could contact? ☞ **Try out one or two first and see what happens.**

4 Ask for introductions

No two people have exactly the same network of contacts. Each person who supports you knows people who you don't know but who might be interested in supporting you. Your supporters will not necessarily think about offering you an introduction to these people but, if prompted by you, they might well be willing to make the connections.

You may feel you've already done this with the list you made for 'throwing the net wider' in Chapter 21. But, like Elijah going back over the same road, it's time to revisit it.

Ideally you are looking for people who you know well, who have already agreed to support you and who have a quite different network of contacts from yours.

You will need to talk this through with your supporters. If you simply ask them, *"Do you know anyone who might be interested in supporting me?"* their minds are likely to go blank, so you may need to prompt with other types of questions, such as:

- Is there anyone in your church with an interest in mission and who might be interested in hearing about my work in Turkey?
- Would your house group, or maybe some individuals in the group, be interested in hearing about what God is leading me into with the Kurdish people?
- Are there any Christians in your work who might like to hear about what I'll be doing with Mid Med Mission? Maybe we could get together for a bite of lunch?

Assuming that the existing supporter does come up with a few suggestions, there are a number of ways in which they can make the connection.

- They contact someone on your behalf and prepare them for your contact. Whether they phone the person or mention it to them in conversation, they do the legwork in setting up the contact for you.
- They suggest someone for you to contact on the basis of their recommendation. This is easier for your existing supporter to do, but is usually less effective. It means that you are the first person to talk to the new contact, albeit using your existing supporter's name as an introduction – a bit like Jim did with Chris. Still, if it's the best you'll get, then take it!
- They host an evening for you in their home where they identify themselves as your supporters and where you explain your ministry. These can be very effective, especially if you have a good way of letting those who are interested in supporting you identify themselves to you.

See pages 225–226 for how to do this.

5 Early increase

Some people who began supporting you when you first started raising your support may be willing to increase their support to help you reach 100 per cent. This is especially the case if you have been working on your support for several months, if you are getting close to your target and if the person's interest in you and your work has grown since they first started supporting you.

It could be a house group member who was new to the group when you first talked about your work and your need for support, perhaps six months ago. They signed up for £15 per month at the time but the two of you have since got to know each other much better. Sometimes they will offer to increase their support to bring it into line with your developing friendship. But more often they won't take the initiative, so you will need to.

Example: Claire

Let's assume that Tracey from Westside Community Church in Liverpool started supporting Claire following the evening that Claire's friend from college days had organised for her. There had been no previous contact between Tracey and Claire, but Tracey had been impressed by what she'd heard that evening and had started supporting Claire at £15 per month.

However, it was one of those relationships that clicked and they have kept in regular contact during the intervening four months. By now it is January. Claire has stopped teaching to concentrate fully on her support and the other bits and pieces she has to sort out before going to her orientation week in Cyprus and then on to Turkey. She is due to fly out in three weeks, but still has £130 per month to find. Mid Med Mission are quite strict about reaching 100 per cent of your support target before they will let you leave. While Claire isn't panicking yet, she is beginning to get nervous. £130 per month still to go and only three weeks left. Time for some serious praying, some creative thinking and some decisive action.

She phones Tracey, explains her situation and asks her if she could help in two ways. First of all, does she know anybody else who might be interested in supporting her? Secondly, would she be able to increase her support? She says that she's asking a number of key supporters who have been a special part of her support-raising if they could increase their support.

How would Tracey feel? Given how their relationship has grown over the past four months and that she would now count Claire as a friend, not just a missionary she supports, she is likely to want to help if she can. After all, she has been praying that Claire would reach her support target and now she has the opportunity to help see her prayers answered. My guess is that Tracey would double her support. With the extra £15 plus Gift Aid, that would bring Claire almost £20 per month closer to her target. And it would bring Tracey the satisfaction of knowing that she's helped her friend get that much closer to getting on the plane.

☞ **Take time now to review those who have been supporting you from the start.** Who has shown special interest in your plans and support-raising? Explain your situation to them and ask if they can help get you a bit closer to your target.

By working through these categories of people, not only will you be closer to your support target, you will have begun to discover more of those who God has selected to support you. Hopefully you will also have learned to look beyond the obvious, to look from a different perspective and will have begun to see some resources that didn't appear first time down this road. You will also have branched out into some totally new networks of contacts – and there's no knowing where these will lead to.

Phyllis and I tried to work out how far our links have spread out over the years. As far as we can work out, we have got fifth link supporters. These are people who were introduced to us by someone who was introduced to us by someone who was introduced to us by someone who was introduced to us by an original contact who we already knew! If we had just stopped at the obvious, at the relationship that was already there, we would have missed out on some vital support. We would not have some of the close friends we have today and we would have lost out on enjoying God's surprises.

☞ **Take some risks. Step out beyond what you see with the blinkers on and see what happens. It made a difference to Elijah's life and it can do the same for yours.**

Checklist for when the well runs dry

Loose ends
- ❏ Go back over the contacts where there's unfinished business
- ❏ Check for those people who have a form that they haven't returned
- ❏ Check for any other 'blockages'
- ❏ Contact them again

The forgotten excluded
- ❏ List those you know you have not approached
- ❏ Switch positions: how would you feel if they were raising support and contacted you?
- ❏ Get in touch

Who's new?
- ❏ Make a list of the people you've met for the first time in the past month
- ❏ Apart from the fact that you've only just met, is there any reason not to contact them about supporting you?
- ❏ Get in touch

Ask for introductions
- ❏ Identify supporters who have a different network of contacts from yours
- ❏ Ask them if they know people who might be interested in supporting you (use clear suggestions of where these people might be)
- ❏ Suggest:
    - they contact that person
    - you contact them
    - they host an evening to meet them

Early increase
- ❏ Think about those who have supported you from the start
- ❏ Has anyone shown special interest in your plans and support-raising?
- ❏ Explain your situation and ask them to help you get closer to your target.

CHAPTER 24

Establishing a Prayer Team

A spiritual battle

We are involved in spiritual warfare. This is just as true during the time when we are building up a support team as it is during any other time of our ministry. Having people pray for us very regularly and specifically is the greatest weapon we have in this conflict. [Read 2 Corinthians 10:3-5 and Ephesians 6:18-19] It is also a great source of encouragement to us. And it is the greatest ministry someone can have in our lives.

Of course, we want everyone on our support team to be praying for us. But usually God raises up a few people who will really commit themselves to pray for us on a daily basis.

Individuals as prayer warriors

Choose some people (probably between three and ten) who know you well and have a close walk with the Lord. Maybe they are already praying for you regularly. See them early during the time when you are developing your support team. Give them your specific needs, goals and schedule. Be sure to stay in regular contact, giving them periodic updates. And let them know when and how God answers their prayers for specific requests. As you progress in your support team development, God will raise up others.

Groups praying for you

Choose one or two groups of people (eg, Church prayer meeting, Bible study group) that you could challenge to pray every week as a group for you, your goals and your schedule. Stay in regular contact with them. Let them know how and when God answers their prayers.

What you might pray for those praying for you

"Lord, increase the faith of those praying for me by allowing them to see their prayers answered." Of course, as God answers their prayers, your needs will be met. But more importantly, those people praying for you will see that the Lord is the God who provides and answers prayer, and their faith will grow.

Positive prayer

Faith pleases God and he answers prayers of faith [HEBREWS 11:6, MARK 11:24]. Phrasing your prayer with the positive expectation that God will answer will help you pray in faith. You might want to write your goals for developing your support team as prayers in this positive way and pray them daily.

CHAPTER 25

Keeping it Going

If you've got this far, you will hopefully be well on your way to having your support raised. At the very least you will have a few initial supporters already signed up.

Maybe it's time to take a break and go out for a meal to celebrate God's goodness! You might even bring a supporter along with you as a treat for them.

And this brings us to the next stage in the whole process. **How do you keep building long-term relationships with supporters once they've signed up?**

Each person is different and each set of relationships with supporters is different, so there's no 'one-size-fits-all' formula. However, there are some key principles to guide you as you build your own way of communicating with your supporters.

Tithe your time

You haven't raised support to spend all your time building partnerships with your supporters! You've raised support to allow you to show and tell God's love to people in need, whether directly or indirectly. However, developing good partnerships with your supporters isn't an optional extra in this process. Nor is it something you do to allow you to do your work. It is an integral part of your work.

☞ **As a general rule, you should set aside ten per cent of your working time to communicate with your supporters.** Think of it as an investment of your time – an investment that will pay good dividends both in your work and also in the lives of your supporters.

How you use this time will differ widely from how someone else will use theirs. For example, if you live reasonably close to many of your supporters, then it is easier to meet up with them from time to time. If you are going abroad, then you might spend more time writing notes and sending emails. You might also come back to your home base for a couple of years to spend some concentrated time seeing supporters.

Keeping in contact with supporters is far too important to get relegated to something you'll do next week when things are a bit less hectic. Next week has just come!

Budget for it

Keeping in touch with supporters doesn't just deserve an appropriate slot in your diary, it also deserves an appropriate slot in your budget. ☞ **Make sure that you factor the cost of creatively keeping in touch with your supporters into your support target.** Depending on your support target and how far away you live from your supporters, you should assume that it will cost you around five per cent of your total support target to pay for prayer letters, phone calls, sending birthday cards, buying little gifts for some supporters, and so on.

If you are working with an organisation, check how much they have built into your support target for support maintenance. If the answer is 'nothing' and there is no other source of funds in the organisation to cover these costs, ask if you can raise an extra five per cent for the cost of keeping in touch with your supporters. And if you are working independently, add an extra five per cent to your target.

In Egypt the Israelites were forced to make bricks without straw – it didn't work very well. Make sure that you have whatever resources you need for the bricks that will build your wall of financial and prayerful support.

More than just prayer letters

For many people who live on support, the prayer letter or newsletter is the basic way of keeping in touch with their supporters and other friends.

This works well as a good way of maintaining basic contact with a large group of people. But prayer letters don't communicate as well as, or as much as, you'd like them to. Remember that this is the family of God at work as givers and receivers. **A family where one set of siblings communicates to the other set using only impersonal letters every few months isn't likely to function that well!**

Be consistent and creative

A former colleague of ours used to say, rather pragmatically, *"Out of sight, out of mind. Out of mind, out of money. Out of money, out of ministry!"* Whatever plan you develop to build and maintain relationships with your supporters, make sure that there is plenty of activity in it. Your supporters, whether individuals or groups, have their own lives, their own busyness and their own priorities. With the best will in the world, they don't get up every morning with you at the forefront of their mind. It's not that they aren't interested, it's just that they need help from you to bring their interest to the front of their minds. The more you can communicate with them, the more likely it is that some of them will respond through additional financial support, prayer and encouragement.

☞ **Once you've finished reading this chapter, use the page at the end to begin putting together a plan that will allow you to be consistent in communicating with your supporters.**

Add creativity to your consistency. If your communication isn't creative, it slides into predictability and you can end up losing the interest of your supporters.

More for some; less for others

Not everybody needs, nor appreciates, the same level of contact. Someone with a high commitment to you and your work needs a very different package of communication compared with someone on the fringes of your life, who maybe signed up for your prayer letter after you spoke at an event and from whom there has been absolutely no contact since then. You have a finite amount of time and money to use to keep in touch with people, so invest more in those who have a higher level of commitment to you. These may or may not be your highest financial givers, but they will be the people who have demonstrated the most commitment to you.

Let's assume that you send your prayer letter to 200 people. Within this you are likely to have three categories of people:

- First of all, the 130 or so whose commitment to you is, at best, limited. For them a prayer letter every few months, perhaps along with a Christmas card or some other type of personal contact once a year, is sufficient.

- Secondly, the 50-60 who have some **higher level of interest** – perhaps they support you financially or have expressed some specific interest in you and your work. For them, **try to have some form of personal contact (postcard, note, personal email, etc) every three to four months in addition to your prayer letter.**

- Finally, the 10-20 people who are **vital to your support team**. These are your key people, the ones who really do see themselves as an integral part of your ministry. **For them, try to have some type of personal contact every month.**

As the months and years pass, **you will need to develop some sort of promotion and relegation process in your communication.** It is no help to them to keep dumping a high level of communication on the person that you really thought would be interested, but who hasn't replied to any communication and who hasn't asked you an intelligent question about your work in months. Conversely, the person who may not have seemed that interested at the start but who now is showing a high level of interest needs to hear more from you in the future.

Making it Work

Don't forget the children

If you have families supporting you, ☞ **don't forget to communicate with the children**. Birthday cards, postcards from places you visit, maps of the country you work in, photos of people you work with, these all help develop an interest not only in you, but might even excite them about a life of Christian ministry. It will also bless the parents in helping them to instil the values of God's Kingdom.

And finally…

The one who calls you is faithful and he will do it.

[1 THESSALONIANS 5:24]

Creative ways of keeping in touch with supporters

See if you can come up with 30 different ways of keeping in touch with your supporters and involving them in your ministry. Start with categories that fit your context – eg, items to post, practical involvement options, social activities together, prayer contact, useful gifts in kind, contact with their children. Then list as many creative individual ideas as you can think of.

1.
2.
3.
4.
5.
6.
7.
8.
9.
10.
11.
12.
13.
14.
15.
16.
17.
18.
19.
20.
21.
22.
23.
24.
25.
26.
27.
28.
29.
30.

Building a support maintenance plan

You are more likely to keep in good contact with your supporters if you plan it into your diary. At the start this might need to be a conscious decision; but eventually your contact with supporters should become just as natural as any other aspect of your work.

To help you get started, begin to build a plan around the following:

What can you do every day?

Pray for two supporters

-
-
-

What can you do every week?

Write notes to two supporters

-
-
-

What can you do every month?

Check if any new people have sent in a gift

-
-
-

What can you do every quarter?

Send a prayer letter

-
-
-

What can you do every year?

Send a small Thank You gift to key supporters

-
-
-

Keeping it going

SUMMARY

Here's a brief summary of some of the main things we've talked about in Section 3…

Getting going
- Make sure you are constantly praying about all aspects of your support-raising and are having others pray for you too.

Drawing up a list of contacts
- How many fish are in your sea?
    - List all the Christians you know or who know you.
    - Add your family members.

Who tops your list?
- Number the people on your list 1–6, according to the decision-making ladder (p.73).
- Concentrate on the middle categories on your list.
- If God allowed you just one supporter, who would you want?
    - Highlight their name.
- Who would the next five be?
    - Highlight their names too.

Getting sorted
- Keep an up-to-date record of everybody on your list.
    - Use a simple card-index file to note down contact details and record appointments made, follow-up, etc.

Arranging to meet up
- Choose someone to contact from your list.
- Give them a quick phone call to arrange a time to meet up.
    - Explain that you want to talk to them about your support, but don't get dragged into long explanations yet.

Planning what you're going to say
- Think about the information your potential supporter is looking for (p.167).
- Gather people-stories to explain what your work will be about.
- Write your support presentation (p.182).
- Get a friend to practise on, or practise saying it out loud in front of a mirror.

Summary continued...

When you meet up
- Keep the flow of conversation natural and informal.
- Keep the conversation focused.
- Speak from your heart, not from your script.
- Take some promotional material with you.
- Be sure to have standing order forms and Gift Aid Declaration forms with you.
- Agree a time when your potential supporter will get back to you with their decision.
- Agree a time when you will get back to them if you haven't heard from them.

After you've met up
- Send a thank you note within a day.
- If your potential supporter doesn't get back to you when they said they would, ring them.
- Remember it may take a number of re-contacts to get to the point where the potential supporter actually completes the process. Keep the initiative.

Contacting people by letter
- If you can't arrange to meet up, write a personal letter, explaining what you would otherwise tell them face-to-face.
- Follow it up with a phone call.

Talking to people beyond your core group of close friends
- Prepare a visual presentation album (pp.200–204)
- Practise using it with a friend.

Raising support from churches
- Talk to someone in your church leadership as soon as possible about your plans.
- Find out about the rules governing mission-giving in your church.
- Start talking to groups as soon as possible about what you hope to do.
- Appoint an ambassador to act as your link with the congregation.
- Book the spare bed and get people thinking about coming to visit you.

Summary continued...

Throwing the net wider
- List other Christians you know who have a different network of contacts from yours (p.217).
- Think about how possible introductions might work.

Speaking at regular meetings
- Remember these are good places to give information but not always to raise support.
- Take copies of your standing order form and Gift Aid Declaration form just in case.
- Give everyone a brochure or some other information about your work that includes a response form.

Speaking at special meetings organised to hear about your work
- Make sure the host is already a supporter.
- Make sure the people invited know you will be talking about your support needs as well as your work.
- Pass out lined index cards to everyone at the end.
    - Ask them to put their contact details and a tick if they would like to consider being part of your support team.
- Ring the ones who tick their card within 48 hours.

When the well runs dry
- Remember Elijah – and go back over ground you think you've already covered.
- Work your way through Chapter 23 and the checklist on page 238.

Establishing a prayer team
- Ask some key friends to pray for your specific needs, goals and schedules.
- Choose one or two groups of people to pray for you.
- Let them know how and when God answers their prayers.

Keeping it going
- Set aside ten per cent of your working time to communicate with your supporters.
- List creative ways of keeping in touch with your supporters (p.246).
- Build a support maintenance plan (p.247).

Odds and Ends

Funding Your Way Through Bible College

Whether it is by doing a three-year theology degree course or a cross-cultural mission course lasting a few months, it is quite normal for people going into Christian ministry to choose to get some training before they jump in at the deep end. Almost all Bible colleges in Britain have a good cultural mix, with students from all continents represented at most of the major colleges. Being exposed to such a global view of life and Christian ministry can be a great help, whether your plans will take you across the world or just across the city.

As you explore the option of attending a Bible college, you will soon realise that the normal funding principles of adult education and training don't apply. Normally, people who do some course of study or training hope to get a better-paid job at the end of it. But the majority of those going through Bible colleges will have a worse-paid job at the end of their studies than they had before they started!

To compound matters, you may also find that the normal funding principles of mission support don't apply either! I don't know why it is, but some churches, especially those with limited involvement in supporting missions, struggle to see training for ministry as being a valid call on the church's funds. This is especially true if the student isn't sure about what they will do after their studies and is using his or her time at Bible college to test their way forward in God's plan.

So, where does this leave you?

Student loans

They can help – if you can get them. But you will need to consider how you will pay off this debt in subsequent years, especially if your income sits just above the repayment level. And if it is many years until your income is high enough for you to pay back your loans, are you comfortable carrying around this level of debt?

Once you're OK with the implications of repaying the loans then, by all means, see what is available. They are only available for certain types of courses, in certain types of colleges to certain types of students. And the rules change from time to time. Ask the college you are applying to if you might qualify. They should be in a position to explain all that you need to know.

Loans can help a bit. But there's a better option. Keep reading…

Part-time job

You could get a part-time job for a few hours each week during your college course. Squeezing in an outside job during a full-time course can work for some. But it inevitably means something else gets squeezed out – spending time with other students, being able to get back home as often as you'd like, meaningful involvement in a church near the college, perhaps even your studies. Be careful about trying to fit in so much that you lose out on some of the hugely important relational aspects that sit around the fringes of college life. You may never get a chance like this again.

Income from a part-time job can help a bit. But there's a better option. Keep reading…

Savings

You are well advised to start saving towards your training for ministry as soon as you even begin thinking about it as an option. If you are going to ask others to support you from their available money, it shows integrity if you are prepared to put some of your hard-earned cash into the process as well. It might even mean you choosing to postpone going to college in order to build up some more funds.

However, for the reasons listed below, it isn't necessarily a good idea to fully fund yourself through your training. You will need to judge whether you should postpone your training for ministry so that you can build up more savings. And you should certainly not choose this option just because you don't want to approach people for support.

Savings can help a bit, but there's a better option. Keep reading…

Developing a financial support team

Raising support for your time in college will give you much more than just money.

Through it you will:

- **attract prayer support** – people who invest financially will pray for you
- **receive emotional support** – it is a great encouragement to know there are people interested in you right at the start of your venture into Christian ministry, even if you're not sure what your training might lead to
- **develop a support-base early** – at the end of your studies you are likely to live on a support basis for several years, and at a much higher level of financial need than you will have at college. What better time to start the process than when you have a relatively small need for a defined period of time. Raising support also helps keep your friends involved in your life as you prepare for a life in Christian ministry

- **encourage a mission vision in your church** – the best recruiter for Christian work is someone already involved, especially someone just starting out who many existing members already know well
- **stretch your faith** – we grow by doing things that are not easy
- **learn new skills** – as you raise support for your training, you will develop communication skills that will be very useful to you in the future.

Your best sources of good supporters are your church and your friends. They are the people interested in your life to date and they are those most likely to want to invest in your future. If your church shows little interest in helping support you during your studies, you will need to work even more on your friends.

Your church

Right at the outset, even before you apply, ☞ **talk to your pastor or church leader**. I am part of the leadership of my own church and we are delighted to see anyone in the church showing an interest in any form of Christian ministry. But it doesn't help if the first we hear is when the person has already made a decision and hopes that the church will pay for it. Give your church leaders the chance to explore the options with you from the outset.

☞ **Understand the church policy for support and ask how to be considered.** Work with the leaders on how best to present your ministry to the church. Getting the congregation personally involved gives them the opportunity to support someone they know well.

Sometimes a smaller support group within the larger congregation can be key in bringing your prayer and any other needs to the wider church.

Your friends

People enjoy giving, even if you feel uncomfortable receiving! ☞ **Make sure that you give those who know you the chance to get involved in your future.**

Often unexpected people will want to support you. ☞ **Pray about who to ask.** Who is on your Christmas card list? What about neighbours or former neighbours, old school friends, former churches? If you could only have one supporter for your time at college, who would it be?

☞ **Start with that person**, sit down with them, explain what you plan to do and why and ask them if they would like to be part of the great adventure God is leading you into.

☞ **Then choose the next two or three… then the next few.** Soon you will have a group of keen givers and prayers committed to helping you fulfil what God is calling you into. If you can't get to see them in person, send them a handwritten letter saying the same things.

While non-Christians can't pray for you, some may want to support you financially. This is also a great opportunity to talk to them openly about your relationship with God.

Keep it going

☞ **Make sure that you keep in good contact with your supporters while at college.** Letters, postcards, emails, phone calls and visits all build the partnership with supporters that makes this much more than a simple money matter. Also, write a short thank you note within 48 hours to those who give you a gift.

Produce a factsheet

It can help to have a creative factsheet to give to your church, friends and relatives. Even better if it has good pictures in it!

- The opening sentence should grab attention
- Then update your life story
- Share your motivation so the reader gains a sense of your call
- Describe your future ministry and the training you will receive
- Include your financial needs
- Provide a way to respond.

Keep track

☞ **Keep a record** of who you have asked and their response and aim to reply quickly to any offers of support, making sure they know how to get the support to you.

Pray

☞ **Pray that the Lord will work above your plans.** Pray for the right words to say. Pray for your supporters and their lives. Prayer should underpin all the points listed above.

Odds and Ends

Resources

If you need a way for people to be able to give tax-efficiently to you while at college, ☞ **contact Stewardship** (www.stewardship.org.uk). They have a special arrangement that allows them to reclaim tax through Gift Aid payments from supporters who are UK taxpayers, increasing the payments by 28 per cent!

Extra expenses

As you go through your training, especially if it is more than just a few weeks, you may face some additional and perhaps unexpected costs. These could range from a placement to some distant land for a few weeks to replacing your old laptop that finally crashes. ☞ **This is a good opportunity to contact people to ask for a special gift.** And don't avoid those who have already given. They are the people who are most likely to want to help with whatever the special need is.

> **Steve and Deb's story:**
>
> We knew that God wanted us to go to college to prepare for full-time Christian ministry. We also knew that we would need financial support to do this. Thankfully we had a good group of friends who were excited by our plans and wanted to be part of it. First we asked a couple in our church we knew well if they would co-ordinate our support group. They had outgoing personalities and were delighted to help. We then approached other friends and built up a core group of supporters, mostly from our church, but also including friends from other aspects of our lives.

Our church gave us support from the church budget and also allowed individuals to give to us through the church. Our support group held fundraising events like car boot sales and promise auctions. They also helped in other ways – gifts of food, family days out and helping with our children. A Christian trust also gave a small grant towards our expenses.

We did end up living on a tighter budget than before, but this was easier than we'd thought. And, yes, God did look after us – and very well too!

Keeping Your Spiritual Perspective

Being filled with the Spirit and spending time with the Lord is essential at all times, of course. Since support-raising often creates particular spiritual stress, we dare not neglect our walk with the Lord.

Walk in the spirit

Do not take being filled with and walking in the Spirit for granted. As in all aspects of your life, make sure you keep short accounts with God, confessing sin when necessary and walking in close fellowship with him at all times. We can never afford the luxury of carnality and this is especially true while developing your support.

Maintain a daily quiet time

Working on your support can keep you very busy. Even if you do have free time, there is a tendency to let other activities crowd out your daily personal time with God in his word and in prayer. **Make sure you plan this time into your schedule every day.**

Many have found it best to study sections of the Bible that look at God's character, promises and his calling.

The next pages outline a series of Quiet Times specially prepared for your support development time. Unless you have a better Quiet Time programme already in operation, take time to work through these on a daily basis.

Praise and thank God often

It is a good idea to spend time regularly in praise and thanksgiving. Not only does God command it, but it will lift your spirit and cause you to really focus on how great and loving God is. You might want to try listening to tapes of praise music, using a hymnal, or reading Scripture passages of praise to God, as means of praising him.

And remember to thank the Lord for his provision to you and for the ways he is conforming your character to that of Christ during your support-raising.

Some suggested passages to read and pray back to God as praises:

PSALMS 18, 21, 22, 33, 66, 67, 92, 100, 111, 117, 148, 149, 150

REVELATION 4, 5, 9:9-12, 15:1-4, 19:1-6; 2 CHRONICLES 6-7; 1 CHRONICLES 29

ISAIAH 9:1-7, 40, 42:5-13, 55; DANIEL 2:19-23; EPHESIANS 3:14-21

1 TIMOTHY 1:17 LUKE 1:46-55, 67-79, 2:13-15

Spend a day with the Lord

Getting away every now and then for an extended period of time of study, worship, praise, reflection and prayer is an excellent way to renew your energy and perspective, as well as seeing the Lord encourage your heart. Doing this can be especially helpful if your support-raising time is lengthy.

God's Character and Provision: some study outlines

These outlines provide different reading and meditation suggestions - seven dealing with God's character and six with God's provision. You may want to alternate the 'character' and 'provision' passages, spend two or three days considering some of the longer passages, or intersperse these studies with your existing Bible study programme.

God's character

Read each of the following passages and note any aspect of God's character you find. Complete the sentence, 'God is...' in a few words.

Meditate on the verses and your description of God's character.

Then describe how you have seen this aspect of God become real in your life during this past year.

1. ISAIAH 6: 1-5

    God is...

2. 2 SAMUEL 7: 18-29

    God is...

3. NUMBERS 23: 18-20

    God is...

4. PSALM 139: 7-12

    God is...

5. 1 John 4: 7-21

   God is...

6. Lamentations 3: 19-24

   God is...

7. Isaiah 40

   God is...

God's provision: Philippians 4:10-20
When someone gives – everyone benefits

The Philippians had sent gifts to Paul on occasions to at least three different locations: when he set out from Macedonia; when he was in Thessalonica; and, finally, when he was in Rome. Not an easy thing to do when there were no postal services or bank transfer facilities. Their commitment to giving was so great that they overcame these obstacles. In the end, they probably benefited more from giving the gift than Paul did by receiving it (vs 17+19).

ACTION POINT: Add your written responses in the space provided.

How did the giver benefit?

How did the receiver benefit?

How did God benefit?

Thank God for the benefits being shared by you, your supporters and by God himself through his faithful provision.

Keeping your spiritual perspective

God's Provision: Exodus 16
God provides – in spite of us

This is one of the classic passages of scripture relating to God's provision for his people. Throughout the chapter there are two contrasting themes: God's unfailing faithful provision; and the Israelites' grumbling, disobedient response. In spite of the response of the people, God provided manna for 40 years.

Imagine how much more pleasant reading this chapter would have been if the Israelites had been trusting and grateful rather than grumbling and disobedient.

As you look at your income this month, do you thank God for the £1 that someone gave or grumble about the £1,000 that didn't come in as you expected?

Do you really trust God to meet your needs, even on the days when no 'manna' arrives (v.27)?

Because God loves us, he **will** provide for us whatever our response. But let's make it easier all round by being trusting, grateful receivers.

ACTION POINT: Take some time to think through your attitudes towards God's provision. List below any areas of grumbling or disobedience and replace them with prayers of trust and gratefulness.

Odds and Ends

God's Provision: Matthew 6
He who worries doesn't trust - he who trusts doesn't worry

The sermon on the mount makes refreshing reading in a society so dominated by an attitude of 'Get all you can while you can' (and give yourself ulcers while you do it!). Jesus' teaching stands out like a cool drink on a hot day. VERSE 6:33 sets the pattern for the Christian: set God's Kingdom as your priority and he will look after the rest.

However, this chapter also raises some questions that we need to answer in relation to our own attitudes. Think through those and ask God to change any areas that need changing.

- If God shows me a need to meet, what do I do and how do I do it?

- Where am I storing up my treasure? (If in doubt, check where your heart is – that's where your treasure is.)

- What am I seeking first – God's Kingdom or my support?

ACTION POINT: From verses 25-34 list as many reasons as you can why we should not worry about clothing, food, etc.

Keeping your spiritual perspective

God's Provision: Exodus 35-36:7
The 'more-than-enough' story

The story so far in Exodus is mostly one of God outlining to Moses the patterns of worship for his people, while they ignore him or disobey him every chance they get. God has now decided to provide a more visible presence of himself with the Children of Israel. In spite of all he has done for them, they need something tangible to stop their minds from wandering away from him – just like we need the communion service to ensure we don't forget what Christ has done for us.

Moses explains to the people all that God had outlined to him regarding the plans of the tabernacle and he asks them to give what they can to pay for its construction.

Do the people respond?

Just take another look at 36:3-7. – They gave so much that Moses had to stop them giving any more!

I wonder if Moses felt nervous when he launched his fund appeal for the tabernacle. After all, it was not very long before this that the people had used their jewellery to make a golden calf, which they worshipped. Imagine Moses' joy when he had to say, 'Enough, no more – you've given more than is needed'.

ACTION POINT: *Take a look again at this passage and see if you can find at least ten principles about God's provision and man's need to give. Here are a few to get you started:*

1. When God's people have their heart moved they will give (35:21)

2. God's people want to be part of his work (35:20-29)

3. God expects a high standard of excellence for his work (35:5-9)

4.

5.

6.

7.

8.

9.

10.

Now that you have found these principles, think through how they relate to the development of your support team. You are doing God's work, as he commanded, and his people are providing what you need to do it. Maybe the day will come when you have to say to your supporters, "Enough, no more - you've given more than I needed!"

God's Provision: The Book of Haggai
God owns it – be careful how you use it

In previous passages in this section we have looked at God's provision in spite of us, his total commitment to us, his fatherly concern for us, and the benefits that come from his provision. In this passage we see what happens when people lose sight of who the provider is and misuse the provision.

The people of Haggai's time had spent a lot of time and money building their own houses – obviously to a very high standard. But in the process they had neglected the Lord's house, which lay in ruins (1:4). God had prompted them to reconsider their priorities by affecting the prosperity of their business and agriculture. They "planted much, but harvested little" and earned wages "only to put them in a purse with holes in it" – and we thought inflation was a modern phenomenon!

But the people still paid no attention. So God eventually intervened directly through Haggai and gave instructions about the rebuilding of his house. By then it had been so long since any attention had been paid to the temple that Haggai had to ask, "Who of you is left who saw this house in its former glory?" (2:3)

However, as soon as the people turned their minds back to God's priorities, God began to restore their earlier prosperity (2:15-19).

It is good to build a habit pattern of gratefulness for all God provides and to be careful to ensure that we recognise the importance of the **provider** rather than the provision.

ACTION POINT: Make a list of all the things you own which you would find difficult to give away. As an act of trust and commitment, ask God to accept the ownership of these items (after all, he already owns them) and allow him to use them to the best advantage of his Kingdom.

God's Provision: Genesis 41:53-42:28
(if you have the time, read the whole story 37:1-50:26)

When the only light at the end of the tunnel is a train coming to get you

The story of God's provision through Joseph is one of the most fascinating in scripture. Imagine Joseph's despair, confusion and fear when, as a teenager, he was sold by his brothers and ended up as a slave in a country whose customs and language were foreign to him. Not only that, but he was imprisoned – apparently indefinitely – for something he didn't do.

Yet, about 20-25 years after his brothers sold him to the travelling Ishmaelites, Joseph was responsible for preserving his family's life during the famine and so protecting the lineage of the Messiah. As Joseph looked back over his life, he commented to his brothers, "You intended to harm me, but God intended it for good to accomplish what is now being done, the saving of many lives".

ACTION POINT: List any situations in your financial support team development that are confusing you, causing you fear or tempting you to despair. Thank God that even if you don't understand what's happening, he does and he will work it out for good. Then do as Joseph did: continue to honour God and trust him not only to provide for you, but through you to provide for the needs of others.

Notes

Useful Contacts

Global Connections

Global Connections is an expanding network of evangelical agencies and churches that are involved in mission from, to and in the UK. Our vision for the network can be expressed in the statement, "Mission at the heart of the church, the church at the heart of mission".

Until 1999, Global Connections (GC) was known as the Evangelical Missionary Alliance. GC has always been independent of the Evangelical Alliance, but we regard ourselves as sister organisations. At the time of the name change, Global Connections moved from being an alliance of world mission agencies working outside the UK, to becoming a network of all the stakeholders in global mission connected with the UK.

As a membership organisation, Global Connections links nearly 200 agencies and colleges and a growing number of churches. We serve the network by organising forums, providing an information service, running conferences, circulating resources, facilitating training events, producing discussion documents, initiating surveys and offering financial services. We aim to keep at the forefront of mission thinking on behalf of all our members.

Global Connections links the evangelical mission network in the UK with the EEMA (European Evangelical Missionary Alliance) and with other mission networks on every continent of the world.

In 2006, Global Connections launched a completely revised and redesigned website which is seen by us to be a vital tool for uniting, networking, training, informing and encouraging the whole evangelical mission network in the UK.

> Global Connections
> Whitefield House
> 186 Kennington Park Road
> London   SE11 4BT
>
> Tel: 0870 774 3806
> Fax: 0870 774 3809
> Email: info@globalconnections.co.uk
> Web: www.globalconnections.co.uk

Stewardship

sovereign account
for christian workers

A message from Stewardship

Stewardship are delighted to have helped Myles Wilson as the publishers of this book. We hope that his teaching has imparted something of God's heart for your ministry, as well as practical ideas to help build your supporter base.

Another way in which we help those in Christian ministry is through the Sovereign Account. This is an excellent way to organise your support and increase funds by nearly 25%. Contact us to find out more.

stewardship

Strengthening your support.

An account designed to enhance both the relationship with your supporters and the value of their support.

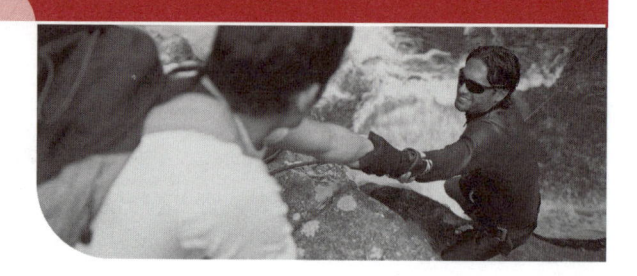

tel:
08452 26 26 27

email:
enquiries@stewardship.org.uk

web:
www.stewardship.org.uk

Together we can make a difference

Join together with one million other Evangelical Christians to transform society.

Through the **Evangelical Alliance** your voice will be heard and your ministry resourced.

Evangelical Alliance UK
Whitefield House, 186 Kennington Park Road, London SE11 4BT.
Tel 020 7207 2100 Email info@eauk.org
Registered Charity No. 212325

evangelical alliance
uniting to change society

These organisations have been helpful to others, offering advice and resources covering a wide range of issues in Christian ministry. Depending on your situation, you may find one or more of them helpful to you also.

Association of Christian Financial Advisers (ACFA)

Provides a directory of a wide range of financial advisers who subscribe to the Evangelical Alliance's statement of faith and who are in good standing within their community.

☎ 01474 853777

🖱 www.christianfinancialadvisers.org.uk

Christian Research

Undertakes and publishes research on a range of trends and issues that can be a help to people in Christian ministry.

☎ 020 8294 1989

🖱 www.christian-research.org.uk

Christian Vocations

Provides advice and information about vacancies in Christian organisations.

☎ 01384 233511

🖱 www.christianvocations.org

Credit Action

Provides a range of resources and publications to help with money problems and other stewardship issues through written materials, seminars and telephone helpline and online debt advice.

☎ 01522 699 777

🖱 www.creditaction.org.uk

CWR

Offers counselling and pastoral leadership training.

☏ 01252 784 700
🖱 www.cwr.org.uk

Equip at Bawtry Hall

Offers training in intercultural ministry and leadership.

☏ 01302 710020
🖱 www.equiptraining.org.uk

Ichthus Motor Mission

Offers loans of vehicles at special rates to missionaries belonging to Christian mission societies, as well as to ordained Christian ministers, who are not normally UK residents and who accept the Evangelical Alliance Statement of Faith.

☏ 020 8291 5144
🖱 www.ichthusmotormission.com

Interhealth

A medical charity providing specialist health services to aid, development, NGO and mission organisations.

☏ 020 7902 9000
🖱 www.interhealth.org.uk

Lawyers' Christian Fellowship

Can offer referrals to Christian solicitors who may be able to advise on legal issues.

☏ 01246 856783
🖱 www.lawcf.org

OSCAR

Information, advice and resources for anyone involved or interested in Christian work around the world. Includes a whole section on finance.

☎ 0845 257 6315

🖱 www.oscar.org.uk

Stewardship Forum

An Evangelical Alliance initiative bringing together a group of Christian organisations and individuals who share a vision to see Christians better equipped to understand why and how to give effectively. Some good online resources.

🖱 www.stewardshipforum.org